Stephen M. Griswold

A Woman's Pilgrimage to the Holy Land

Stephen M. Griswold

A Woman's Pilgrimage to the Holy Land

ISBN/EAN: 9783337293758

Printed in Europe, USA, Canada, Australia, Japan

Cover: Foto ©Lupo / pixelio.de

More available books at **www.hansebooks.com**

A

WOMAN'S PILGRIMAGE

TO THE

HOLY LAND;

OR

PLEASANT DAYS ABROAD.

BEING NOTES OF A TOUR THROUGH EUROPE AND THE EAST.

BY

Mrs. STEPHEN M. GRISWOLD.

WITH NUMEROUS ILLUSTRATIONS.

SULTAN'S CIPHER.

HARTFORD:
J. B. BURR & HYDE.
1871.

Entered according to Act of Congress, in the year 1871, by
STEPHEN M. GRISWOLD,
In the Office of the Librarian of Congress, at Washington.

CASE, LOCKWOOD & BRAINARD,
PRINTERS AND BOOKBINDERS.
Cor. Pearl and Trumbull Streets,
HARTFORD, CONN.

As a Token of Love

TO MY AFFECTIONATE SON

FREDERICK,

I Dedicate This Volume.

INTRODUCTORY NOTE.

BOOKS upon travels will be written to the end of time.

It has been my privilege, in company with my husband, to visit most of the palaces, cathedrals, and galleries of art in Europe, and the mosques and ruins in the East. The route of our journey was through England, France, Switzerland and Italy, where we joined the memorable " *Quaker City* excursion party" to the East.

We remained with them about three months, during which time we visited Constantinople, the Black Sea, Sebastopol, Smyrna, Ephesus, the Holy Land, and Alexandria, Egypt. There we parted from them, and taking one of the Austrian Lloyd steamers to Corfu, from thence we sailed through the Adriatic Sea to Trieste, visited the great Cave of Adelsberg in Austria, and crossed the Styrian Alps to Vienna.

INTRODUCTORY NOTE.

We returned through Central Europe, down the Rhine and across the German Sea, to Scotland and Ireland.

It was our good fortune to see most of the crowned heads of the Old World, including the Queens of England and Prussia, Napoleon III., Eugenie, the Pope of Rome, the Sultan, and the Viceroy of Egypt.

In company with the excursionists we visited the Emperor and Empress of Russia at their summer residence on the shore of the Black Sea.

During the journey I kept a daily record of passing scenes and incidents, not intending it for publication; but at the urgent solicitation of many friends, I have consented to publish it, trusting that its perusal may prove a pleasure to the reader, as its writing was to the author.

G.

PUBLISHERS' PREFACE.

FOR the preparation of this interesting and instructive volume, the authoress was peculiarly fitted by her previous culture, for making the best use of the singularly fortunate circumstances which conspired to give her an opportunity to enjoy advantages which do not come within the reach of the ordinary traveler. Starting from New York and landing in England, her social position gave her access to many things which are out of the reach of the general tourist in that aristocratic island. Passing through England, France, Switzerland, and Italy, she then joined the excursion party of the *Quaker City*, and remaining with them about three months, visited Constantinople, the Black Sea, Sebastopol, Smyrna, Ephesus, the Holy Land, Alexandria, and Egypt. Then leaving the *Quaker City* party on their return, she went to Corfu, through the Adriatic to Trieste and through Austria, crossing the Styrian Alps to Vienna. Returning through Central Europe she passed down the

Rhine, and crossed the German Ocean to Scotland. After a tour through the interesting scenes which the magic of Sir Walter Scott's pen has made household words throughout the world, she passed through Ireland, and took a steamer at Cork for New York. In as brief a sketch as this, nothing but the barest outline of her route can be given. For the descriptions of the interesting scenes she passed through, and the accounts of the distinguished persons she met: for the womanly insight into the social condition of the nations she visited and her sketches of their history and political organization, the reader must consult the volume itself. It is possible here only to assure them that they will never regret so instructive and interesting a use of their leisure time.

ILLUSTRATIONS.

QUAKER CITY OFF THE COAST OF SYRIA.—FRONTISPIECE.	
THE ROYAL EXCHANGE, LONDON,	27
RECEPTION DAY AT BUCKINGHAM PALACE,	30
TOMB OF NAPOLEON,	38
FONTAINEBLEAU, FRANCE.	49
PALACE OF ST. CLOUD,	53
COLOSSEUM, ROME,	100
CASTLE OF ST. ANGELO, ROME, (text),	103
ITALIAN PEASANTRY,	110
NAPLES BAY,	113
NAPLES WAGON,	117
NEAPOLITAN FLOWER GIRL,	119
ERUPTION OF VESUVIUS,	127
TURKISH ARABA,	150
TURKISH BOYS,	156
MOSQUE OF SULTAN ACHMET, CONSTANTINOPLE.	160
MUEZZIN CALLING TO PRAYER,	164

WHIRLING DERVISHES,	168
ROCK-CUT CHURCH OF INKERMAN,	171
ODESSA, RUSSIA,	175
RUSSIAN DROSKY, (text),	177
MERCHANT OF SMYRNA, (text),	196
COUNTRY MOSQUE IN ASIA MINOR,	194
ARAB SCHOOL BOY, (text),	207
CHAIN OF LEBANON,	212
WOMAN OF JAFFA,	221
NIJEM, OUR DRAGOMAN,	226
A TURKISH HOUSE IN JERUSALEM,	239
HOLY SEPULCHRE,	246
INTERIOR OF THE MOSQUE OMAR,	257
JERUSALEM,	265
BETHLEHEM,	281
SACRED GROTTO, (BETHLEHEM),	285
DEAD SEA,	287
PILGRIM'S FORD—RIVER JORDAN,	297
VICEROY'S PALACE,	324
GRAPE GATHERING IN AUSTRIA,	342
SCENE ON THE DANUBE,	346
CONVERSATIONSHAUS, BADEN BADEN,	366
STRASBOURG CATHEDRAL,	372

CONTENTS.

CHAPTER I.
Over the Sea, - - - - - - - 17

CHAPTER II.
England and her Queen, - - - - - 21

CHAPTER III.
France, - - - - - - - - - 33

CHAPTER IV.
Paris and Napoleon, - - - - - - 38

CHAPTER V.
Switzerland, - - - - - - - - 52

CHAPTER VI.
Crossing the Alps, - - - - - - 59

CHAPTER VII.
The Midnight Ride, - - - - - - 64

CHAPTER VIII.
Italy, - - - - - - - - - 68

CHAPTER IX.
Venice, "City of the Sea," - - - - - 73

CHAPTER X.
Milan and Genoa, - - - - - - 80

CHAPTER XI.
Leghorn and Florence, - - - - - 85

CHAPTER XII.
Rome, - - - - - - - - - 93

CHAPTER XIII.
From Rome to Naples, - - - - - - 107

CHAPTER XIV.
Vesuvius and Pompeii, - - - - - - 126

CHAPTER XV.
The Pilgrims, - - - - - - - 135

CHAPTER XVI.
Athens, - - - - - - - - - 140

CHAPTER XVII.
Constantinople, - - - - - - - 145

CHAPTER XVIII.
The Sultan and the Mosque, - - - - 150

CHAPTER XIX.
On the Black Sea, - - - - - - 168

CHAPTER XX.
Visiting the Emperor of Russia, - - - 179

CHAPTER XXI.
Our Stay at Yalta, - - - - - - 185

CHAPTER XXII.
Smyrna, - - - - - - - - - 191

CHAPTER XXIII.
Ephesus and its Ruins, - - - - - 199

CHAPTER XXIV.
From Smyrna to Syria, - - - - - 203

CHAPTER XXV.
Lebanon, - - - - - - - 208

CHAPTER XXVI.
Jaffa, - - - - - - - - 216

CHAPTER XXVII.
Starting on the Pilgrimage, - - - - 224

CHAPTER XXVIII.
Going up to Jerusalem, - - - - - 232

CHAPTER XXIX.
The City of the Great King, - - - - 236

CHAPTER XXX.
Within the Holy City, - - - - - 242

CHAPTER XXXI.
The People of Jerusalem, - - - - - 249

CHAPTER XXXII.
The Temple, - - - - - - - - 255

CHAPTER XXXIII.
The Turkish Family, - - - - - - 262

CHAPTER XXXIV.
Outside the Walls, - - - - - - 269

CHAPTER XXXV.
Mount of Olives and Bethany, - - - - 275

CHAPTER XXXVI.
Bethlehem, - - - - - - - 280

CHAPTER XXXVII.
The Dead Sea, - - - - - - - 288

CHAPTER XXXVIII.
River Jordan, - - - - - - - 296

CHAPTER XXXIX.
Bedouin Arabs, - - - - - - - 303

CHAPTER XL.
Return to the Ship, - , - - - - 309

CHAPTER XLI.
Egypt, - - - - - - - - - 314

CHAPTER XLII.
Leaving the Pilgrims, - - - - - - 322

CHAPTER XLIII.
The Voyage, - - - - - - - - 329

CHAPTER XLIV.
Cave of Adelsberg, - - - - - - 336

CHAPTER XLV.
Vienna, - - - - - - - - 344

CHAPTER XLVI.
Salzburg and Munich, - - - - - - 353

CHAPTER XLVII.
Baden Baden, - - - - - - - 362

CHAPTER XLVIII.
Strasbourg, - - - - - - - - 373

CHAPTER XLIX.
Down the Rhine, - - - - - - 378

CHAPTER L.
Cologne, - - - - - - - - 388

CHAPTER LI.
Brussels and Waterloo, - - - - 395

CHAPTER LII.
Antwerp and the North Sea, - - - - 403

CHAPTER LIII.
Scotland, - - - - - - - - 409

CHAPTER LIV.
From Scotland and Ireland, home, - - - 418

CHAPTER I.

OVER THE SEA.

AS we cannot cross the ocean in an American steamship, we take passage on a steamer carrying the English flag. The wharf is crowded with people, bidding good-bye to their friends, who are about departing on a voyage to the Old World, along with us. Among the crowd are our friends who are waiting to wave their last adieu. The anchor is up, our moorings unloosed, the bell strikes, the ship's gun sounds the farewell, and we sail out of New York harbor. Now come the mingled thoughts of pleasure and sadness, with memories of those left behind; but I am about to realize what I have always ardently desired, a visit to foreign lands.

I am roused from my reverie by the sound of the

gong summoning the passengers to dinner. Here we gather, both young and old, about one hundred and fifty persons, and how full of life and anticipation they seem! Seated opposite is an English clergyman and his family. He is a specimen of a strict minister of the church of England, and is already making friends among his fellow passengers. His wife is a portly old lady, weighing not less than three hundred pounds. We have on board several clergymen; among them a Catholic bishop on his way to Rome, also a noted General, and his wife, who are on their way to Italy to spend the coming winter.

Immediately after crossing the bar at Sandy Hook, the steamer commenced rolling and madly plunging, upsetting things generally. A heavy northeast gale continued two days and nights, during which it was impossible for any of the passengers to remain on deck. After the third day, it cleared beautifully, and the ocean seemed at rest.

The days passed on much after the fashion of the others, until on the afternoon of the eleventh day out, land came in sight. How joyfully that cry sounded over the ship! Our glasses were brought in requisition for a fairer view; and our Captain informed us that we were nearing the Highlands of Galway, Ireland. The sun was setting in all his glory, reflecting a red and purple hue over the sea. A lady, standing beside me, appeared transfixed, so glorious was the scene. She was probably thinking of the loved parents whom she was about to visit, not having seen them for twenty-five years.

A prayer meeting was called on deck, and all joined in singing Old Hundred, in thankfulness for our safety. Our old English lady companion was also impressed with the thoughts of nearing home, for later in the evening, she and her daughter were singing very sweetly "Home Sweet Home."

The next morning we arrived at Queenstown; and after landing passengers and mails for Ireland, we steamed up St. George's channel having Wales on our right hand, soon passing Holyhead. We were awakened very early next morning, and found ourselves at Liverpool. Hastening on deck, we could see nothing but a vast quantity of masts and ships. On our steamer all was confusion, from the general preparing to land. We walked down the gang-plank one by one, where officers stood ready to examine our baggage. This being found all right, we were allowed to pass through the great iron gateway. Very soon, seated in an English cab, we are driven to the Alexandra hotel, where we rest awhile after our voyage.

CHAPTER II.

ENGLAND AND HER QUEEN.

THE first thing we notice is the substantial manner in which everything is built.

Liverpool is a busy city, and contains many fine buildings, the most elegant being the new Exchange.

Of course, we must patronize one of those queer carriages called "Hansoms," and drive along the quay.

Some years ago there was an effort made to introduce the Hansom cab in New York, and doubtless most of the people there have seen them; but many of our readers might like a description. It is a small carriage on two wheels, the driver sitting on a high seat behind. The reins pass over the top of the carriage and fall down over its front to the horses' head. A window closes in front of the passenger, through which he has a fine view of all that is passing in the streets; even though the rain should be falling, he feels cozy and well protected though his poetic dreams may be disturbed by the unobstructed view of the wretched Rosinante which too often does the service for the Hansom cabman.

Thirty miles by rail and we reach Leeds. Here we find the most noted woolen manufactories in England. Not stopping long, we continue on to Manchester, a cheerful looking city, where we are politely guided through the cotton manufactories. The Exchange, during business hours, presents an animated scene, which is well worth a visit.

The Derby chapel in the old Cathedral is interesting. It was built by an Earl of Derby, and one of them is there buried.

Seated in a comfortable railway carriage, we arrive, sooner than I expected, at Rowsley station, where those wishing to visit Chatsworth Palace and Haddon Hall, stop. Here I have my first view of an English inn. How often I have read of such places, and associated with them a bustling landlord, or landlady, stage coaches rattling up to the door, and luggage being taken in. Well, we did not enter this way, but drove up quietly to the quiet old inn. Over the door was the date when the house was built, 1652. Above the date is the coat of arms of the Duke of Rutland, as this was formerly his shooting-box. Our agreeable hostess having provided us with a fine team, we proceed to Haddon Hall. This huge pile of buildings, massively irregular in architecture, once belonged to the Vernon family, but in consequence of the runaway marriage of Dorethea Vernon and Sir John Manners, it fell to the Duke of Rutland. It is now a romantic old ruin, battered and worn by the elements. The whole pile is surrounded with fine old trees that spread in every direction, rich with associations of past ages, and fresh with the most luxuriant growth of nature.

Within is the banqueting hall, the bed of Queen Elizabeth, the state chairs used during the reign of Henry the Seventh, and over the fire place in the private dining room are the words, "Dread God and honor the King." When we were again seated in the carriage I felt amply repaid for my wanderings through this ancient hall. It was the first castellated ruin which I had ever visited.

Going through a pleasant country, and stopping at the little town of Bakewell to purchase pictures, we soon entered the grounds of the Duke of Devonshire's palace, said to be the handsomest private residence in the world On these grounds is the tower where Mary, Queen of Scots, was confined thirteen years. In the park adjoining the palace are thousands of deer. The conservatories are very extensive. Growing in profusion are pine apples, bananas, oranges, figs, lemons, and ginger, also many exotic plants, and flowers from India, Egypt, and South America, among them the marvelous Victoria Regia, one of a genus of water plants named after the queen. It is a native of S. America. Its leaves from three to five feet across, have a rim some four or five inches high; and its white flowers are almost three-quarters of a yard in diameter. The interior of the palace is certainly beyond description. Paintings from eminent artists, statuary from

THE ROYAL EXCHANGE, LONDON.

the most distinguished sculptors of past ages are gathered within its walls.

The Duke owns two other estates in England, besides a house in London and a large property in Ireland. His income is said to be over five thousand dollars a day; and yet, while there is such great wealth in England, there is also great poverty and wretchedness; within a few miles of these elegant mansions, and vast landed estates, are thousands of human beings who are living in want and misery.

From Newstead Abbey, Derby, and Nottingham we find ourselves at Windsor Castle, arriving about ten o'clock in the morning, in company with a lady and gentlemen of the Queen's household, who escorted us through the castle, and very kindly afforded us an opportunity to see the Queen, also Princesses Louise, Beatrice, and Prince Leopold. The Queen is quite plain and unpretending in her appearance, medium height, with a countenance beaming with intelligence and love. She was neatly attired in mourning. The people revere Victoria, but since the death of her husband she has remained so secluded as to give much dissatisfaction to the aristocracy. We feel deeply obliged to our friends for the pleasure which they have rendered us this day, remembering that by their aid we were enabled to see England's Queen. Bidding them adieu we enter St. George's chapel and attend service. The chapel remains the same as when the Prince of Wales was married.

An hour's ride brought us to London, where we remained many days visiting the various places of note in and around the city. Among them St. Paul's Cathedral, Westminster Abbey, the Royal Exchange, Buckingham Palace, Houses of Parliament, Thames Tunnel, Tower of London, and the matchless Sydenham; also parks and gardens, of which there are a great number.

The Royal Exchange is one of the most interesting monuments of London. Sir Thomas Gresham, financial agent of Queen Elizabeth and of her successor, saw, in his frequent borrowing excursions to Antwerp and other cities of the Low Countries, then the financial rulers of the world's commerce,

RECEPTION DAY AT BUCKINGHAM PALACE.

the importance of freeing England from her dependence upon these countries. The first exchange he built at his own expense and presented it to the city of London. That was burned in 1838, and the present Exchange, the proud symbol of England's commercial dominance, stands on its site.

Buckingham Palace, the town residence of the Queen, is of little interest in an architectural point of view. Windsor Castle and Hampton Court are a thousand times more significant; but the interior of Buckingham Palace on a court reception day presents one of the grandest exhibitions of social pomp in the world. The glitter of diamonds and precious stones of all kinds, the display of costly fabrics, the beauty of women, the glitter of royal decorations upon the breasts of men, the sheen of silk stockings, for gentlemen must all wear these or be refused admittance, the gorgeous costumes of the attendants, who stand immovable, holding huge battle axes, emblems of barbarism—altogether form a scene never to be forgotten.

We attended Mr. Spurgeon's church. He is

about thirty-seven years of age, short of stature, rather thick set, dark hair and eyes, and a very pleasant expression. He makes no use of notes, but preaches with a captivating eloquence, that is calculated to do much good.

The days spent in England have been delightful. The people were hospitable and courteous, for which we shall always have the kindest recollections of merry England.

CHAPTER III.

FRANCE.

"ALL ABOARD!" We and our luggage are hurried on a little steamboat; rain is falling, and I am glad to descend into the ladies' cabin. But alas! the accommodations are limited, the room is very small and close, beds are made on the seats, and some on the floor.

I was so amused watching the ineffectual efforts of the ladies to comfortably arrange themselves for the night, that I could not think of sleep. I am not surprised that so many passengers ask the question, why the conveniences on the channel steamers are so inadequate, considering the vast amount of travel between England and France.

It was a tolerably quiet night crossing the channel, and at nine o'clock the next morning we reach

Dieppe, France. The first thing which attracted my attention was the women in white caps, with broad frills. Some were riding on donkeys, others walking, while their donkeys were loaded with vegetables for market. Dieppe is a large city, famous among other things for its unrivaled manufactures from ivory.

In a luxurious French railway carriage whirling through the valley of Normandy to Paris, we passed some of the most beautiful scenery in France. Some parts were a perfect flower garden. There were whole fields of the red poppy, which are cultivated for the oil obtained from its seeds. This oil is much used by the people for salads, many preferring it to the oil of the olive. It is a clear, sweet, and nearly odorless oil. Long rows of Lombardy poplars are planted on either side of every stream of water, extending miles in length. The wood is used to make charcoal, and by engravers and cabinet makers, while its leaves, either green or dry, are readily eaten by sheep and cattle.

After a delightful ride, we entered the city of

Paris. Our first business was to install ourselves in a good hotel, which was not very difficult, as Paris abounds in them.

From my window I noticed people sitting by little round tables, sipping chocolate and chatting away. Presently a baker passed with a large tray of bread made in strips two yards in length, piled up about four feet—this he carried upon his head. Most of the horses that pass have bells jingling about their necks. The drivers seem trying to outdo each other in cracking their whips. Over the smoothly paved streets omnibuses are passing to and fro with as many passengers on the top as there are inside. Those wishing to ride outside, can pass up a little ladder which is attached to the end of the stages. Flower girls walk by with beautiful flowers in their hands, offering them for a few sous. The Parisians are lovers of flowers; not only the rich but the poor have a universal taste for them.

The sidewalks are filled with gaily dressed people walking leisurely as though care or business never troubled them.

I am called from this panoramic view, to visit the cathedral of Notre-dame. Its history is connected with the greatest events of Parisian life. Here the coronation of Napoleon Bonaparte and Josephine took place. It was an occasion of great splendor, the Pope coming from Rome to crown them. Louis Napoleon and Eugenie were here married. It is one of the grandest cathedrals of Europe and dates from 1163, when the first stone was laid by Pope Alexander III.

The church of the Madeleine stands next in importance, built after the style of the Parthenon at Athens, intended by Napoleon to represent the temple of fame, afterwards completed by Louis Philippe. This church has a most grand appearance. It is approached at either end by a flight of twenty-eight steps, and the whole building is surrounded by a colonnade of fifty-two corinthian pillars each forty-nine feet high.

In the morning we take a carriage for a drive in the Bois de Boulogne, passing up the Champs Elysées to the Arc de Triomphe which was commenced by Napoleon first in the year 1806. Within the arch are recorded all his victories and the names of his generals. We ascended two hundred and eighty steps to the summit; here we remained some time enjoying what is considered to be the grandest view of Paris, the whole city lying like a map before us.

Leaving the Arc and riding through the avenue De l'Imperatrice we enter the Bois de Boulogne, the Parisians favorite park and fashionable drive of the *beau monde*. Late in the afternoon we see the ladies and gentlemen driving around in splendid equipages. The wood is charming; there are broad roads for carriages, shaded avenues for equestrians, and lakes with boats upon them. In some of these lakes are little islands on which are beautiful flowers and pleasure houses where delicate refreshments can be obtained.

Night coming on we return to our hotel in time for the *table d'hote*.

CHAPTER IV.

PARIS AND NAPOLEON.

THIS has been a bright July day, and we have improved it by visiting the tomb of Napoleon. Passing up several marble steps we enter a beautiful edifice, called the Domes des Invalides; under the dome rest the remains of Napoleon first, who was brought here from the island of St. Helena, in the year 1840, as in his will he requested that his ashes might repose on the banks of the Seine, in the midst of the French people whom he had ever loved.

The tomb is of Porphyry, weighing over one hundred and thirty thousand pounds. Around the tomb are twelve magnificent statues. Near the crypt is a statue of the Emperor. The cost of the entire building was between two and three million

TOMB OF NAPOLEON.

dollars. The people are constantly coming and going, visiting this illustrious shrine.

Near to this stands the Hotel des Invalides, founded by Louis Fourteenth, as a home for disabled soldiers. We saw the old veterans walking and sitting around, apparently well provided for. They have little gardens for their out of door amusement, and some of these are kept with great neatness and taste. Others look much neglected. Wine is daily furnished to all the veterans, as are also tobacco and snuff for those who use them.

In the top story of the building are models of all the fortified cities of France, made by the inmates, in plaster and wood.

Wending our way to the Rue de Rivoli, one of the busy streets of the city, we are soon at the Place Vendôme. In the center stands the Column Vendôme, erected by Napoleon First to commemorate his German campaign in 1805. It is formed of twelve hundred captured cannon, and the shaft is surmounted by his statue.

In the Place Royale, is the home of Victor Hugo,

and near it that of Richelieu, both ancient looking buildings.

Near by is the Place de la Bastile, where stood the castle in which Marie Antoinette was imprisoned. It was one of the most famous dungeons in the world. In the revolution of '98 the enraged populace razed it to the ground.

The Palais Royal is the residence of Prince Napoleon, Princess Clotilde, his wife, and Prince Jerome. In the garden, which is surrounded with elegant jewelry shops, the lower story of the quadrangular palace being rented for this purpose, we seated ourselves beside the fountain to listen to a band of music which plays every afternoon at four o'clock. Here crowds of people congregate. I often remark they *seem* to have nothing to do but to enjoy themselves and be happy; this is the way it appeared to me all the time in Paris. Their Sundays are not regarded as in America. It is more of a holiday with them, and many of the stores are open, while crowds of workmen with their wives and children seek the fresh air and green fields of

Saint Cloud, Fontainebleau, or other places, in the railway trains leaving Paris at almost all hours.

The finest stores are on the Boulevards, Rue de la Paix, and the Rue de Rivoli, where are to be found the most elegant goods of all description. The sidewalk of the latter is covered by the buildings, forming a long arcade.

The Louvre is very extensive, and requires several visits. The museum of antiquities is on the lower floor. In the Imperial museum are to be seen Napoleon's sword, camp-bed, writing desk, several coats pierced with bullets, his last used gloves, and his state coronation chair, also relics of Maria Antoinette, the jewels of Maria Louisa, and other interesting objects.

Here are galleries after galleries of paintings. In one no pictures are received excepting those whose masters are dead. We quickly sought out Murillo's "Immaculate Conception," which is considered the most valuable of the collection, and by some the finest picture in the world.

Connected with the Louvre are the Tuileries, the

city residence of Napoleon and Eugenie. The interior is fitted up in the most opulent and costly style. The garden of the palace is divided from the Rue Rivoli by a high railing ornamented with marble urns filled with flowers.

The grounds are exquisitely laid out, abounding with statuary and fountains. They embrace an area of fifty acres, and are thronged with people from morning till night on all fair days. There you see the children of the rich from all countries dressed in elegant attire pursuing their juvenile sports. The little sparrows are so tame in these gardens that they often take crumbs from your hand.

The word Tuileries is from *tuile,* a tile, so named it is said because the site was once occupied by a manufactory of tiles of which the roofs in France are quite generally covered. From a window in the centre of the palace of the Tuileries you have a view of which some one says " It is the finest artificial vista in the world. There is a grandeur in the scene from the tops of high mountains, in a limitless expanse of ocean, but standing here and looking up across the fountains and the flowers of the Tuileries gardens, on through the beautiful opening in the Chestnut woods to the grand Place de la Concorde with its costly fountains and its Egyptian obelisk, on still through the Champs Elysées up through the Arc de Triomphe where the eye fails and the Bois de Boulogne which lies beyond is scarcely perceptible, we are compelled to say that we believe there is nothing to rival it in the whole world. It is not only grand, but it charms us with the conviction that if nature is beautiful, nature improved by art is infinitely lovely, because it always excites a higher emotion than that of mere gaping wonder. It challenges our admiration for the achievements of human industry and increases our love for humanity.

This is a great day in Paris, Napoleon is to review his army; early in the morning crowds are wending their way to the Champs Elysées, and mingling with the throng we succeeded in obtaining a favorable position from a window of a café, directly opposite the Palace of Industry, where the Empress Eugenie was seated. One by one the state carriages began to arrive filled with ladies who took seats in the windows of the palace. Ere long, amid the shouts and cheers of the populace, and the music of many bands, surrounded by a body guard of nearly two hundred men, dressed in gorgeous uniforms, Napoleon came riding up the grand avenue, and took his position in front of the Palace of Industry. He wore a look of self-possession, which impressed the beholder. His dress consisted of a gilt helmet with white ostrich plumes, a light military coat, and over the shoulder passed a broad green ribbon. His pants were of red velvet, with a black stripe at the sides. Seated upon a gilt saddle, and bestriding a handsome bay horse, he seemed undisturbed by the scene around him. The firing of cannon announced the approach of the army marching twenty-eight abreast, in close order. They were two hours and fifteen minutes passing, presenting a splendid military spectacle.

Alas, for Napoleon! In a few short days how changed the scene. War with its ruthless hand has torn the crown from thy brow and destroyed thy dreams of glory forever.

Napoleon has done much for France, in beautifying its cities and increasing the prosperity of its people, but they do not seem permanently united, or long satisfied with their rulers.

The history of France has been one of vicissitude.

One of the most delightful days of our sojourn in France was that passed at Versailles, eleven miles from Paris. Here is the imposing palace of Versailles, so famous in history. The cost of the palace and grounds of Versailles has been estimated at one billion of francs, or two hundred millions of dollars. The water for its elaborate fountains is supplied from the Seine by forcing pumps, worked by steam, and the cost of working the fountains for a single hour is something enormous. They are played on the first Sunday of every month. The extensive parks, lawns, terraces and gardens, evergreen trees made to grow in quaint abnormal shapes, statues, vases, render the belongings of the palace alone well worth a visit to the city of Versailles. The Petit Trianon, a royal mansion built by Louis XV., for Madame du Barry, was the favorite residence of the unhappy Marie Antoinette, queen of Louis, XIV. This mansion, and also the Grand Trianon are within the grounds of the palace.

Fontainebleau is another famous palace about thirty miles from Paris. It is a magnificent pile and has been the country residence of the court at different times. Here Napoleon in 1814 bade farewell to the famous "old guard." One of the Popes was confined here, about that time, for a year and a half. The palace is rich in paintings by Del Sarto, Da Vinci, Benvenuto, Cellini, and others, but many of their works are falling to decay. The forest of Fontainebleau contains over 34,000 acres and is perhaps the finest in France. The illustration represents one of its magnificent, shaded avenues beside the largest of its beautiful lakes.

Saint Cloud is another of the famous palaces of France. The village of Saint Cloud, containing something over three thousand inhabitants, is about

FONTAINEBLEAU, FRANCE.

five miles west of Paris. In 1782 Louis XVI. purchased it for Marie Antoinette, and since then it has been a favorite residence of the royal family, especially with the two Napoleons. On Sundays, at least, and on other days for ought that I know to the contrary, the populace are permitted to roam all over the beautiful grounds of Saint Cloud, and hundreds of their children may be seen sporting or rolling upon its thick green grass, or wandering around its cool lakes. When there are such luxuries within the reach of the poor workmen, is it a wonder that he takes his wife and children to enjoy them even on Sunday, the only day on which he can leave his workshop?

CHAPTER V.

SWITZERLAND.

S T. CLOUD, Fontainebleau, and many other interesting places, in and around Paris, and the delightful day spent at Versailles, finish our sight-seeing at Paris, and we must leave for other scenes of interest.

The next morning we proceed to the *gare*, or railway station, by seven o'clock to take the cars for Basle, Switzerland. Riding all day, a distance of three hundred and twenty-five miles, going through the Champagne districts of France, by dark we reach Basle, and putting up at the hotel de la Couronne we partake of a good supper and retire to our room fatigued after the long ride of the day.

The next morning much refreshed we start out to explore the place.

PALACE OF ST. CLOUD.

Basle is situated on both sides of the river Rhine, and is a decidedly ancient looking city. The people speak German. A new Protestant church has recently been erected at great expense, the money having been left for that purpose by a rich merchant of Basle.

We leave by rail for Lucerne. The scenery along the route is characteristic of the country. Here the picturesque Swiss cottage is seen, the roof so far overhanging the house as to afford a perfect protection to its sides, under this projection we frequently see suspended herbs and vegetables.

Every canton has a different style of cottage, and all are curious objects to the traveler.

Arriving at Lucerne we take rooms at Schwanen Hotel. This place is the capital of the canton, and is very prettily situated at the head of the lake of Lucerne, the river Reuss dividing it into two parts. The peasantry are remarkable for their costume. The women, wearing a short skirt, with white waist, and very full sleeves. Over the waist is a black bodice with shoulder straps. The old women wear long braids of hair hanging down their backs, are usually bare headed, sometimes with a handkerchief tied over the head, or a very singular looking hat with the front turned up.

The people seem to be industrious and happy. The prominent objects of interest are the three bridges over the river Reuss, decorated with strange looking pictures, representing different phases in life, and the " Wounded Lion " from a model by Thorwaldsen. This is a monument erected in memory of the Swiss guards, who fell at Paris in 1792. A remarkable feature is the beautiful spring of clear water at the foot of the monument. Below its surface you see a perfect reflection of the figure above, which is carved out of the side of a high rock.

We went out sailing on the lake. It was calm and pleasant, not a ripple stirring its surface. Near a small island, we came to a large bed of pond lilies, growing in profusion. They were the largest and loveliest I ever saw. We gathered our arms full, and on the way back suddenly a shower came on, obliging us to take shelter under an old boat shed; but we were quite thankful to get even that, as the rain fell in torrents. Near by was a poor Swiss cottage from which the children would come running out to peep at us, and then dart back into the cottage to tell of the strangers. The shower soon over, we sailed back with our boat load of lilies. Nearing the town the sound of the bells came softly over the lake, it being the custom to ring the chimes every hour. With good appetite we enjoyed an excellent dinner, and afterward took our seats upon the balcony of the hotel. The view is magnificent. On the right stands Mount Pilatus; opposite across the lake Mount Rigi, their tops covered with snow. Far in the distance, peak after peak of the Alps can be seen, with the everlasting glaciers resting between them. The sun sinking in the west, casts its departing rays upon the Alpine snow and ice, and a bright rainbow appeared, only to vanish and give place to another; and as the light faded slowly away, we were lost in admiration. Our thoughts went out in praise to the great Artist who is able to paint such a glorious panorama. Gradually the scene changed and the full moon came up over Mount Rigi, casting her silvery light upon the placid waters of the lake. A boat shoots out, and takes its place about one quarter of a mile from the shore. A band of musicians is on board and there they remain discoursing sweet music, until far into the hours of night. This afternoon and evening in Switzerland will never be effaced from my mind.

CHAPTER VI.

CROSSING THE ALPS.

AT four o'clock in the morning we are called "to take a *gong* through the lake." A small narrow steamer is ready, and in a few minutes a little company of travelers are gathered on deck and the bow is pointed toward the other end of the lake. The first stopping place was Weggis, where quite a number disembark to ascend the Rigi. They were well prepared with broad-brimmed straw hats, coarse heavy shoes, with sharp nails in the soles, and the *alpenstock* in their hands. I noticed written on a staff belonging to one of the gentlemen, the names of the different mountains that he had ascended, among them were Mounts Blanc and Vesuvius.

The air is pure and bracing, and the mountains

become more lofty and grand as we speed along the clear waters. We cannot think of going below to our breakfast, as we should miss the changing scenery. A little table is set upon the deck, over which the Swiss maid spreads a white cloth and on it places delicious honey, for which Switzerland is noted; bread, cheese, eggs, and a good cup of coffee complete the meal.

High up the mountain sides could be heard the tinkling of bells where the herds were feeding, and perched on the sides almost to the very edge of the snow, were to be seen the little summer huts of the shepherds. As the season advances and the snow melts, they drive their flocks higher and higher, coming down at the earliest approach of autumn, bringing their summer manufacture of butter and cheese.

The lake of Lucerne presents to the traveler the most sublime scenery in Switzerland. The mountains reaching to the clouds on either side, their tops white with snow, present a scene of wild grandeur impossible to describe.

This is the land of William Tell, all the surroundings are immortalized with his fame. We are pointed out the spot where he leaped ashore and escaped from Gesler. A chapel to mark the place has been erected, and once a year mass is celebrated here, whither the people repair in boats decorated with flowers.

The Swiss believe in William Tell, and venerate his name. The masses would not probably receive with any complacency the reduction of their favorite hero to a mythical legend; and yet if we believe such scholars as Delapierre, Cox, and others, the first mention of the name occurs some four hundred years before the pretended historical William Tell came upon the scene. It is further significant, to say the least, that there is, in history, no mention of the tyrant Gesler.

Arriving at Fluelen, a town situated at the end of the lake, we find the diligence in which we had engaged passage before leaving Lucerne, all in readiness to set out on the journey over the St. Gothard, one of the most awe-inspiring of the Alpine passes.

The diligence is a clumsy looking vehicle with three apartments. Each passenger takes the seat assigned him by the number on his ticket. Drawn by four horses, we commenced the mountain ascent, passing, after a short distance, the statue commemorating the place where "Tell" shot the apple from his son's head.

The road was very good and quite smooth. Our traveling companions in the stage were an English lady and her husband, both quite sociable and diverting. All day long we were winding up the mountain, the view becoming more wild and rugged. We halted at the little town of Andermatt, and soon after setting out again, we passed the bridge under which the Reuss plunges and roars in an awful manner. This bridge was the scene of a terrible struggle between the French and Austrians in the year 1799.

Often times the road would lie along the very edge of a precipice, down which no one could scarcely dare to look. On the opposite side of the chasm, streams of water came leaping over the sides of the cliffs, and falling through the air thousands of feet. Numbers of these cascades are to be seen. They are caused by the melting of the glaciers.

The poor horses strained every nerve as they endeavored to draw the heavy carriage up the zig-zag course. Away down in the valleys we saw flocks of sheep, chamois and goats feeding.

The Alpine flora are exquisite. Several times during the day, the gentlemen would jump out of the diligence while in motion, and gather beautiful bouquets of flowers delicate in odor and form and brilliant in hue, which had grown and blossomed among the snows. As the afternoon wore on we rapidly neared the top. The air became piercing cold, snow and ice all around, bringing into requisition all our extra clothing. As the way became more steep, the number of horses were increased until twelve powerful ones were pulling with all their might. Two o'clock, three o'clock, four o'clock, and we stand on the top of St. Gothard, almost eleven thousand feet high, with the clouds rolling far beneath our feet.

CHAPTER VII.

THE MIDNIGHT RIDE.

WHILE the driver is changing horses, an opportunity is afforded us for rest and refreshment, and we have ample time to examine the celebrated Hospice of St. Gothard. There are several of these hospices built on the Alpine passes, to provide for travelers. They are inhabited by monks, who keep dogs, trained to rescue lost wayfarers who often miss their way in the blinding storms which frequently occur. Within ten miles of where we are, four rivers rise, the Reuss, Rhone, Rhine, and the Ticino.

The view is now truly sublime. As far as our sight can penetrate from the lofty point on which we stand, hundreds of snow capped peaks are seen piercing the deep blue sky. East and west extend the Alps in the form of a great crescent, bounding the north of Italy. Here is the home of the glacier, and the terrible avalanche. How insignificant the works of man appear compared to the awful grandeur of this scene!

The call of the driver announced " all ready," and bidding the old monks a hasty good bye, we hurried into the diligence. There were only two horses now attached. The driver with his feet firm upon the breaks, gave his whip a loud crack, the horses started on a gallop and the descent commenced. This is the most fearful part of the ride. The road often turning abruptly, you have the sensation that you are going over the edge of the precipice, thousands of feet into the valley below. Glancing down the head becomes dizzy, and we turn away with a fevereish and helpless sensation, trusting to the driver, and the safety of the breaks. Passing a number of small villages, about eleven o'clock at night we reach the town of Bellinzona. Here a crowd collected around the diligence to hear what news there was, for the arrival of the stage appeared quite an event to them. The people looked differently from any which we had seen, more like Italians.

Our English friends unexpectedly concluded to remain in Bellinzona rather than undergo the midnight ride, notwithstanding the fact that there was no room for them in the inn.

Just before starting two men dressed in Italian costume entered the stage and took seats opposite. One of them was armed with a rifle and a sword. These were to be the only passengers beside ourselves.

For two weary hours we were winding up another chain of the Alps, when suddenly a terrible thunderstorm broke upon us, peal after peal crashed through the mountains, echoing from crag to crag, until the very earth trembled. As the continual lightning flashes illuminated the midnight darkness, the two passengers could be seen, one apparently watching us, while the other was feigning sleep. A feeling of fear took possession of me, and I prayed for the light of day, and deliverance from this lonely ride. The hours seemed days. At three o'clock the storm passed away, and the moon came out, somewhat dispelling the gloom. We were now riding along by lake Lugano where another passenger was added. We were glad for any relief from the loneliness of our situation. As the morning approached the air began to feel more sultry, and as we descended upon the plains of Italy, daylight revealed to us that we were passing through Italian villages. Beggars came running after us, some of them rolling like a hoop along the road, expecting a few pennies to be tossed out to them. After a long delay at the custom house, our baggage being closely examined, we were allowed to proceed. Passing a few more towns, about nine o'clock we drive into Como. The time from the Lake of Lucerne, was twenty-six hours, during which time there had been required six drivers and forty-eight horses to our diligence.

CHAPTER VIII.

ITALY.

I WAS glad enough to get out of the old diligence, and know that I was in classic Italy. We were landed in the middle of the street, with our baggage set beside us. Presently we saw running toward us a miserable looking old man, who looked at us, said something, and pointed to the baggage. We perfectly understood his gesures. He left us but returned quickly with a hand cart, into which he threw the trunks and started off, while we followed bringing up in front of the hotel De l' Ange. A very large room was assigned us, with a marble floor and frescoed ceiling. The windows opening on a stone balcony, commanded a fine view of the lake, so romantically associated with Bulwer's play, *The Lady of Lyons.*

After a visit to the Cathedral, and Broletto, the

next day we take the steamer through the lake of Como to Lecco. The view is varied and enchanting. Among the most charming villas to be seen, is the "Villa d'Este" once the residence of Queen Caroline of England, also "Villa Montebello" where Napoleon and Josephine resided after the fall of Venice. Caroline, queen of George IV., it will be remembered, was offered a pension of fifty thousand pounds on condition that she would never return to England. She rejected the offer with contempt and arriving in England in the summer of 1820, she was received by the people, who never withdrew their allegiance to her, with acclamations of joy. A charge of unfaithfulness was brought against her, which though never substantiated as a fact, created much scandal, and the following year when George the Fourth was crowned in Westminster Abbey the doors were closed against her. The people did not perhaps believe her entirely guiltless, but they would not place reliance upon any charge emanating from a husband who had treated her with revolting cruelty.

I had often desired to see this noted lake, but it far surpassed in beauty my expectations, and yet while its shores are lined with orange and citron groves, its lovely villas, its magnificent situation among the Alps, it lacks one element of beauty, the three hundred and sixty-five lovely islands of our own bewitching Lake George.

The steamer reaching Lecco about two o'clock in the afternoon, all the passengers were compelled to march into a fumigating room, where dishes were placed on the floor, filled with chlorid of lime, also something in a vial to inhale. After remaining in this room until we were almost suffocated with the dense smoke of something burning, we were allowed to leave. The weather was very warm and this fumigating was a sanitary measure to prevent any of the passengers from bringing infection into the city. Lecco is a small place not affording much to detain the traveler, so we proceed to Bergamo, and from there to Verona, arriving at midnight. The road leading to the city presented a fine appearance in the bright moonlight being broad and well shaded with trees.

The gates of the city of Verona we found closed; but soon an officer came, and after scrutinizing us, opened them and we were driven to the hotel Tour De Londres.

Verona is an interesting city, built on both sides of the river Adige, which is crossed by four stone bridges. Its wonderful fortifications must have cost as much money as it required to build the city itself.

It is noted for being the birth-place of Paolo Veronese, or "*Il pittor felice*," the happy painter.

Bright and early we were off with our *cicerone*, visiting churches and cathedrals. Going through a convent, then across a garden having on one side a high stone wall, we came to a small old building. In this our guide naively pointed out with much satisfaction "*La tomba di gieuletta la sfortunata*," the tomb of Juliet, the unfortunate. It is made of marble and looks very ancient.

The Amphitheatre is one of the most extraordinary pieces of Roman architecture in existence.

It is supposed to have been erected about the time of Titus. The outside is in ruins while the inside is almost as perfect as when built. There are seats for twenty-five thousand persons, all made of hewn stone, and the places where the wild beasts were confined, and led in and out, are plainly to be seen. We ascended and walked along the great stone seats, Plants and weeds had sprung up and were growing plenteously among the crevices.

From " Verona the Worthy " we continued our journey through a fine country. The fields were covered with wild flowers, and the grape vines running up the trees and hanging from the branches in graceful festoons formed a characteristic part of the scenery.

Going by many Italian villages and cities we approached a large level tract of country, on which tall grass was the only thing growing. Evidently we were nearing the shore; and in a short time we descried, far off upon the water, Venice, the " City of the Sea."

CHAPTER IX.

VENICE, "CITY OF THE SEA."

AT noon we arrived at Venice where again we were subjected to the process of fumigation, with which we have now become accustomed. Afterward we were detained at the custom house, to undergo a rigid examination of our passports and baggage. It is both annoying and amusing, to see how the bags and trunks get ransacked and tumbled, many of them having been packed with care. The officers being satisfied, we were permitted to depart. Stepping out on a platform in front of the custom house we are greeted by a confusion of voices calling " *Gondola signore?* " " *Gondola signore?* " and in a few minutes we are gliding along the grand canal. How strange the scene! No rumbling of carriages or stages, no shouting of horsemen, all is silent, yet thousands in these gondolas are passing to and fro continually. Approaching the " Grand hotel de la Ville " and entering a vestibule with flowers in large vases, and trees growing on either side, we are shown up a flight of broad marble steps, to a room with velvet and rosewood furniture, and oriental decorations. This is called the Turkish room, and opens into a museum containing many curiosities, also great gilt chairs, reminding me of those in the "Houses of Parliament."

Pleasant has been the time devoted to Venice ; it has passed away like a dream. Days were spent, sailing in gondolas in the water streets, also exploring palaces, churches, galleries, and dungeons. If one wishes to step out of the hotel, he must call a gondolier. Some of the gondolas are very elegant, especially those which are owned by the wealthy Venetians. In the days of Venice's greatness they were so extravagantly decorated that the government issued an order for them to be painted black only, and the custom remains to the present day. The only ornament is a broad piece of steel fastened to the prow, polished bright and glistening in the sunlight.

> " Didst ever see a gondola ? for fear
> You should not, I'll describe it you exactly :
> 'Tis a long covered boat, that's common here,
> Curved at the prow, built lightly but compactly,
> Rowed by two rowers, each called a gondolier.
> It glides along the water, looking blackly,
> Just like a coffin clapped in a canoe,
> Where none can make out what you say or do.
> And up and down the long canals they go,
> And under the Rialto shoot away,
> By night and day, all paces, swift or slow ;
> And round the theatres, a sable throng,
> They wait in their dusk livery of woe ;
> But not to them do woeful things belong,
> For sometimes they contain a deal of fun,
> Like mourning coaches when the funeral's done."

At the cathedral of San Marco high mass was celebrated during our sojourn in Venice. The church was thronged in every part; veiled nuns were marching up and down the aisles, bearing lighted candles, while the atmosphere was filled with the perfume of burning incense. Priests dressed in gorgeous robes, performed the service before the high altar. Suddenly a deep silence prevailed, out of which a solitary, mournful, yet sweet voice, was heard singing, far up amid the arches of the cathedral. Soon another was added, the music gradually became more distinct, as other voices mingled, until nearly three hundred singers accompanied by the organ, and a full band of music, swelled the grand chorus, making the service sublime and impressive beyond description.

The Piazza San Marco is the largest open square in Venice, and there every evening a fine band of music plays, while around innumerable little tables are seated the Venetians, enjoying wine and ices, while promenaders pass and repass unceasingly.

One side of the Piazza is bounded by the palace of the Doges. In the great council hall is Tintoretto's "Paradise," next to the largest painting on canvas in the world, being over eighty feet in width, by thirty-five in height. This room also contains the portraits of all the Doges of Venice, excepting one. In another room is the "Last Judgment" of Palma the Younger, a magnificent work of art. The palace is filled with paintings of Titian and Tintoretto, who were both born in Venice.

Leading from the palace to the prison, over the canal, is the terrible "Bridge of Sighs." I shuddered as I walked across, and saw the little window through which many a victim had taken his last look of the light of day.

By the assistance of our *cicerone* and lighted lamps, we proceeded through a dark passage, to the dungeons below; they were small and dismal. If they could speak, what tales of horror would they tell of the tyranny of the secret council of Venice.

The Campanile, or bell-tower, the arsenal, church of Santa Maria della Salute, Santa Maria dei Frari, containing the remains of Titian and Canova, the celebrated bronze horses, brought from Alexandria to Rome, from Rome to Constantinople, thence to Venice, from there to Paris, and after the downfall of Napoleon, carried back to San Marco, are among the wonders of Venice.

Every pleasant afternoon can be seen the upper classes, attired as for a festive occasion, gliding along in their gondolas up and down the grand canal. The social position of the occupant is determined by the dress of the gondolier.

Standing upon the balcony of our hotel one afternoon, the solemn strains of a funeral dirge were heard coming across the water. In a little square opposite was a funeral procession, headed by priests, marching down to the gondola. They approached the water's edge and deposited the corpse in a gondola, which was prepared for the occasion. It moved away followed by several more carrying the mourners.

As soon as the funeral cortége sailed under the Rialto and turned out of sight the band began to play the most lively airs, and the people went on laughing and talking merrily as if nothing had happened, or as if quickly trying to drown the thoughts of death. The procession moved to the cemetery which is on the island of Murano. Here all are buried, the rich and poor, nobles and beggars lying peacefully together.

Our last evening was spent sailing through the different streets and out on the lagoon. We passed several gondolas with hand organs in them, playing very prettily. The scene at night with hundreds of lights sparkling upon the water, and the gondoliers shouting to one another, presents a novel and enlivening spectacle.

CHAPTER X.

MILAN AND GENOA.

MORNING has come, and we must bid good bye to Venice. Taking the early train for Milan, we journey through northern Italy, a very fertile country, well watered with streams from the Alps. Quantities of mulberry plantations are observed along the route, some of the trees entirely divested of their leaves, which have been picked to feed the silk worms. We pass many Italian cities, towns, and villages with their lovely habitations. Lake di Garda, the largest of the Italian lakes, 213 feet above the sea, and famous for its sardines; Solferino, where the allied French and Sardinians fought the Austrians under Francis Joseph in 1859, and gained a victory after sixteen hours of terrible fighting. The French forces were led by Napoleon III., and the Italians by Victor

Emanuel. At Brescia we saw on one of the streets all the fronts of the buildings covered with frescoes, presenting a very quaint appearance.

Here we came across an elderly gentleman with a multitude of bags and bundles, who was returning to America from Jaffa, having been there to investigate the condition of the colony. He was jovial and agreeable, rendering the remainder of our ride quite animated. It afforded a pleasure to meet one that we could converse with freely in our own language.

At the hotel San Marco in Milan, we meet a minister from Massachusetts who had been traveling in Italy over a year for his health. He very kindly served us as a valuable guide through Milan.

This is a clean, well regulated city, containing considerable wealth, and is much visited by Americans. The houses are large and many of them are built of light marble. A wall surrounds the city, in which there are ten massive gates.

The Duomo, or Cathedral of Milan, called the eighth wonder of the world, with its countless pinnacles, is an imposing structure. They led us up nearly two hundred steps to the roof, through the chapels and high arches of the interior and into the subterranean passages underneath, but as this amazing work of art has been so often and graphically described by other writers, I will forego any further description of it.

On the wall of the old convent adjoining the church of Santa Maria delle Grazie is Leonardo Da Vinci's fresco painting of the "Last Supper," painted there by him in the year 1493. He was engaged upon it nearly sixteen years. This painting, to which so many pilgrims have come, is fast going to decay and in a few years will be obliterated. Da Vinci was so fond of trying experiments in the compounding of his colors, that in truth it may be said that his "Last Supper" is slowly eating itself up.

It not being the season of opera in Milan, we obtained permission to visit Il Teatro La Scala, and had it lighted for our benefit. It contains six tiers of boxes hung with crimson and gilt drapery, each one will accommodate from twenty to twenty-five persons. In the rear of each box are rooms for the toilet and attendants. The royal box is situated over the entrance opposite the stage, and is decorated in an elaborate style. La Scala is often called the largest theater in the world, but it accommodates one thousand less than the Bolshoi of St. Petersburg, and seven hundred less than the Academy of Music in New York.

Driving on the Corso we meet many handsome equipages in which are seated the gaily dressed Milanese ladies. The peculiarity of their attire is a black lace veil, worn upon the head and falling on the shoulders. There are many rich palaces in the city. In one is a fine painting of the marriage of Napoleon and Maria Louisa.

From "Milan the Great" to Genoa we have our first view of the blue waters of the Mediterranean, on which we expect to spend much time during the journey.

Genoa "*La Superba*," the proud, is beautifully situated on the shore of the Mediterranean; but like most of the Italian cities it has an old, worn-out appearance. Its streets are very narrow, most of them being only a few feet wide, and the buildings so high that the sunlight scarcely ever reaches the pavement. It is with difficulty we make our way through the narrow alleys crowded with peddlers, friars, monks, beggars and donkeys, to the promenade where the best society of the city is seen.

We meet many of the Genoese ladies with the *mazzro* or head covering of thin white muslin thrown over the head and presenting quite a picturesque effect. It is hard to decide which is the most becoming, the black veil of Milan or the white veil of Genoa.

The city abounds in palaces. One of the most celebrated is the *Palazzo Doria*, so long the residence of the Doria family, one of the most aristocratic in Italy. Among the churches is the cathedral of San Lorenzo, built over six hundred years ago of white and black marble. After inspecting the statue of Columbus, the old Roman wall, and making some purchases at the filigree jewelry stores, we take the steamer for Leghorn.

CHAPTER XI.

LEGHORN AND FLORENCE.

AT Leghorn we became acquainted with the Rev. Mr. Langdon, who was sent from the United States as a missionary to Italy. He made a statement about the religious condition of the Italian people which I will repeat. "There is," he said, "a powerful influence at work to dethrone the Pope, and while Victor Emanuel and Garibaldi take no active part at present, yet they are in sympathy with the movement."

This is a great day in the city, the first iron clad vessel ever built by the Italian government is to be launched. We have a fine view from the windows of the office of the American consul, who is very kind in endeavoring to aid us in every way he can.

The streets, tops of houses, and every available

place are crowded with people to witness the launch. At a given signal the "*Conte Verde*" glides gracefully from her stocks into the water amid the cheering of the people, who were out for a holiday. The women of the poorest class wear handkerchiefs tied on their heads; those in medium circumstances wear a strip of white lace fastened under the chin; only the wealthy ladies wear bonnets.

Leghorn or Livorno, as the Italians call it, is the summer resort of the wealth and fashion of Rome and Florence. The air is pure, without extreme heat or cold, owing to the sea breeze which is almost continuous.

Near the quay is a bronze statue to commemorate the capture of four pirates by Ferdinand 1st.

The Jews have a synagogue which is one of the wealthiest in Italy.

We were accompanied to Pisa and Florence by a lady and gentleman belonging to the *Quaker City* party, and we now begin to meet the excursionists scattered through Italy.

Pisa is a lonely looking city. We drive at once

across the Arno to the Campanile, or Leaning Tower, to the Duomo, Baptistry, and the Campo Santo, which are all clustered near together. Ascending the winding steps of the leaning tower, nearly two hundred feet, until we are fatigued and quite out of breath, we reach the summit of the second wonder of the world. The view is fine, but there is a feeling of fear possessing you that cannot be shaken off; a fear that you are about to fall. The tower has remained in this position many centuries. There are different opinions in regard to its origin and leaning position, some claiming that it was built as it now stands, others that the foundation sunk while the tower was being erected. This opinion is strengthened by the fact that the columns are of unequal length about midway in the shaft, as though there had been an effort to restore the perpendicular. In fact the unequal length of the columns can scarcely be accounted for by any other hypothesis. The tower consists of two circular walls, each two feet thick, and the stairs run up between them. The space or well inside the inner wall is ten feet across. The whole tower is 190 feet high, and is divided into eight stories, each one having a balcony seven feet wide. The top of the column is "out of the true" some fifteen feet; but still it is said that "the line of gravity falls within the base," so we are foolish to have any fear of falling. It may be so, but that does not destroy the instinct of insecurity which is decidedly unpleasant to say the least.

In the Duomo hangs the lamp which suggested the idea of the Pendulum to Galileo when he was eighteen years of age. He was born in Pisa in 1564.

Reaching Florence, we take a room at the "Grand Hotel De l'Europe." This is a lovely city, built on both banks of the river Arno, and is by far the handsomest and most cheerful city in Italy. It abounds in parks and gardens. The collections of paintings and statuary are more varied and ancient than in the Louvre or at Versailles; more of the masterpieces of Murillo, Michael Angelo, Leonardo Da Vinci, Raphael, and Rubens are seen here than at any other place. Days are required to wander through the miles of statuary and paintings in the Pitti palace, the Uffizi galleries, to walk over the gardens, and to examine the royal plate of gold and silver, to say nothing of the libraries and rich museums.

What a terrible history is recorded of the Medici family, who so long occupied this Pitti palace. Cosmo di Medici, called "The Great" and his brother Lorenzo *The Magnificent*, were famous patrons of art and conspicuous as leaders in the republic. Lorenzo opened a garden in Florence filled with antique statuary and devoted it to the use of artists. Among those who availed themselves of this garden was the young Michael Angelo, who so won the admiration of Lorenzo that he took him under his special patronage, giving him rooms in the palace and treating him like a son. Michael Angelo's statue of Lorenzo in the Medici Chapel at Florence is one of the most renowned works of art. The famous Catharine di Medici was the daughter of Lorenzo.

We visited the house of Michael Angelo, still owned by his descendants. It is built of light yellow colored stone, three stories high, with iron barred windows, which is the Florentine style. Within are relics of him and some of his paintings.

Dante's house is very different in architecture, the roof projecting over the sidewalk, and much more antique looking than that of Michael Angelo.

Galileo's villa where he received Milton is also in a good state of preservation. The Cathedral or Duomo with its peerless dome and extraordinarily handsome stained glass windows, the Baptistry with its curious bronze doors which Michael Angelo said were beautiful enough to be the gates of Paradise, the church of San Lorenzo containing the tomb in which are buried the Medici family, the church of Santa Croce where Michael Angelo Buonarotti, Macchiavelli, Galileo, Alfieri, and other illustrious great are buried; the house of Americus Vespucci, the Cascine which is the Bois de Bologne of the Florentines, all came in for their share of attention. We spent a pleasant hour at the studio of the American sculptor Hiram Powers, who has acquired a world wide fame. He is a pleasant unaffected gentleman apparently about 60 years of age, and so cordial in his manner that we felt quite at home while he was entertaining us in his parlor. He then accompanied us all through his studio; among other statues just finished was one of the "Greek Slave," for which he asked four thousand dollars. He had also just completed a bust of his wife and was at work upon one of his daughter.

Mr. Powers informed us that the time was not far distant when he should return to America to spend the remainder of his days.

Passing across the square in front of the Ducal palace one evening, we met a funeral procession which had more of the weird and ghastly about it than any thing I had seen abroad. It was a procession of priests in black masks and long black gowns. As they marched along with slow and measured tread, each bearing a lighted torch in his hand, they chanted a solemn funeral dirge in Latin. The coffin, covered with a black pall reaching nearly to the ground and supporting a large white cross at its head, was borne by the same ghastly masks. A procession of this character in the night in an illy lighted street, is certainly well calculated to strike a vague terror to the heart of the strongest.

Florence excels Leghorn in its alabaster works; in the windows of its numerous alabaster stores which are on almost every street, are seen models of "The Dancing Girls of Italy," "The Three Graces," "The Greek Slave," "The Venus di Medici," "The Apollo Belvidere," and exquisite imitations of the Leaning Tower of Pisa. One of the most curious things in Florence is the *Ponte Vecchio* or old bridge over the Arno. The carriage-way is lined on either side by quaint jewelry shops, and overhead is the famous secret passage or gallery connecting the Pitti palace on one side of the Arno with the Palazzo Vecchio on the other. Another object of interest which we visited was the old Roman wall, now being removed by order of the King. From "Fair Florence," then we turned our steps to Rome.

CHAPTER XII.

ROME.

CIVITA Vecchia, Cervetri, Palo, and we hear the cry "Roma! Roma!" Our passports and baggage being attended to we proceed to the "Hotel de Roma."

Is this the city of the seven hills? "The Eternal City," founded seven hundred and fifty-two years before Christ? Is this the Rome once over fifty miles in circumference, whose empire ruled almost the whole known world? Is this the home of the Cæsars? Are these the streets along which Romulus, Adrian, Nero, Titus, and Constantine, rode in triumph, returning from victorious battles? Yes, Rome, I stand upon thy classic soil, but thy glory has departed. I see the remnants of thy marble fountains, the broken pillars of thy temples and palaces, the ruins of thy Forum, the decaying forms of thy arches, thy Coliseum, Pantheon, monuments, and broken walls all pointing to thy ancient power and splendor.

These are thoughts which crowd upon my mind, as I go from place to place, in modern Rome.

We have comfortable apartments at the Hotel de Roma and good fare. It was at this Hotel that the Empress Carlotta, wife of the unfortunate Maximilian, remained while visiting the Pope for advice, and consolation in her time of grief. The landlord with much pride shows to his guests the suite of rooms which she occupied.

Several *vetturini* or hackmen are ready every morning, each one anxious to be engaged for the day. It is an old saying, that there is a church in Rome for every day of the year, thirty thousand priests, and as many beggars. We soon began to believe in the truth of the saying, for everywhere we went, priests and beggars were to be seen in great numbers. The beggars are very persevering. Some meeting with success in obtaining a few copper coins, would rush around the corner, and take their place on another street, and confronting you with voice and look changed, importune with all the energy of their first attack, declaring that they had never seen you before. The lazzaroni are up to a thousand tricks.

There are about six thousand Jews in Rome, inhabiting a part of the city, called the Ghetto. They were formerly much oppressed by the Romans, but now greater liberty is granted them. They trace their ancestry back to the prisoners which Titus brought to Rome from Jerusalem, in the first century of our era.

As every stranger visits St. Peter's first, we will not be an exception to the rule. Entering the " *Piazza di San Pietro*," the eye sweeps around a a vast colonnade of over three hundred and sixty columns, surmounted by statues. Crossing the piazza by the Egyptian obelisk, with a fountain on the right and left, we approach St. Peters. Over the entrance are immense statues of Christ, and the twelve apostles. Ascending the steps, and pushing aside the heavy curtain in front of the door, we enter, and stand for some time contemplating the immensity of the interior of a structure, costing over one hundred million dollars. Numerous chapels, diverging from the main aisle, are filled with altars and paintings. The lofty ceiling is richly carved and gilded. There hang the pontifical keys. As we approach the high altar beneath the great dome and over St. Peter's grave, on the right is the statue of St. Peter. We see a procession of people passing the statue, each one stopping to kiss the great toe which is almost worn away, although made of bronze. Often could be seen a beggar, performing the ceremony, perhaps the next in turn an elegantly attired lady, who would take out a a highly perfumed handkerchief, and wipe the toe, before putting her lips to it. All seemed to go away with the consciousness that they had performed a sacred duty. Arranged around in the side aisles, were a large number of confessional boxes, each one containing a priest and penitent, while several would be waiting their turn to confess their sins.

One is impressed with the vastness of St. Peters

when standing on the marble pavement below, but even more while ascending to the dome.

Next in importance is the church of St. John Lateran, so called from the Senator Plautius Lateranus, put to death by Nero. The popes are crowned in this church. It contains the tomb of the present Pope, which he has ordered built at great expense. Near the Lateran are the Holy Stairs, up which can be seen people ascending on their knees.

In the church of Maria Maggiore, is a painting of the "Virgin and Child," by St. Luke; it looks very old and the figures are just discernable by the aid of our opera glasses. The frame is composed of the most precious stones. This painting was carried by Gregory the Great, through Rome, at the head of a procession, to stop a terrible plague that was raging during his reign.

One cannot fail to be impressed with the thought while gazing upon these great structures filled with the mostly costly works of art, that it is a great waste of money while thousands of the citizens of Rome are sunk in ignorance and poverty.

One fact tells loudly of the decadence of Christian Rome or of bad management under the Popes. While there have been so many hundreds of millions expended upon the churches in former times, the government of the present day is not able to raise money enough to keep them in repair!

St. Paul's church or the "Tomb of St. Paul," outside of the city, I must not include in the above. It is built of many varieties of the most beautiful colored marbles, and contains the portraits of all the Popes, executed in mosaic. This building is in perfect repair, and is the finest tomb in the world. Near St. Paul's gate is the Pyramid of Caius Cestius, and the tomb of Shelley bearing the inscription "*cor cordium*" or "heart of hearts." After the burning of his body in the presence of Leigh Hunt, Lord Byron, and other friends, the heart of the poet, it is said, was found among the ashes perfect and entire.

We next visited the Flavian Amphitheatre or

COLOSSEUM, ROME.

Coliseum, dedicated by Titus in the year 80, on which occasion according to Eutropius, five thousand wild beasts were destroyed. Dion places the number at nine thousand. This gigantic structure was capable of holding from eighty thousand to one hundred thousand spectators. It is in an elliptical form, five hundred and ten feet broad and six hundred and fifteen feet long. The arena itself is two hundred and eighty-one feet long by one hundred and seventy-six feet wide. Around this arena countless thousands have assembled to see their fellow beings torn to pieces by wild beasts! The gladiators have met here in fierce combat, their life's blood ebbing away amid the shouts and huzzas of the multitude. I call to mind one scene, as I stand within these mouldering walls.

It was a holiday in Rome in the fifth century. Gathered from all parts of the city, until the seats of the Coliseum were crowded, are the fairest and best of Rome's society. Seated in the imperial box, with his nobles around him, is the good king Honorius, who had just arrived, with Stilicho his victorious general.

The gladiators enter the arena, and the conflict commences. One after another is slain. Death-like silence prevails, while two are in deadly conflict. Suddenly a stranger enters the circle, and springing between the powerful combatants, wrests their swords from their hands and becomes master of the arena. Turning toward the imperial box the interrupter of the spectacle, Telemachus a monk, began to address the Emperor, calling upon him in the name of a christian people, to cease such bloody scenes. A howl of rage went up from the assembled throng, as they hurled upon him a shower of stones. He fell to the earth, again and again he attempted to rise, but was beaten down. At last he slowly and with a mighty struggle raised himself and turned toward Honorius, but could not speak. He sank back upon the ground, dying with a smile upon his countenance, as the last words which he heard was the solemn declaration of the Emperor in the presence of his God, that this was the last of such scenes which should ever be witnessed in Rome; and this martyr the last who should fall on the arena of the Coliseum.

Rome is so rich in monuments of its ancient splendor that it is difficult to decide—not what to describe, but what to leave out of any general description of the city. The Castle of St. Angelo deserves mention certainly. It is a citadel whose

CASTLE OF ST. ANGELO, ROME.

center or nucleus was the tomb of Hadrian, and it now serves as a state prison. It is connected with the palace of the Vatican by a long covered gallery.

I will not delay to pen a description of the Pantheon, built in the year twenty-seven by King Agrippa, in which lie the remains of Raphael; the Mamertine prison where St. Peter was confined; the Quirinal; the Pope's summer palace; Hadrian's Villa; Cæsar's palace on Palatine Hill; the Appian Way or the Vatican with its four thousand rooms, its vast number of statues and other sculptured treasures of ancient art. What a thrilling interest they awaken in one when wandering among them! In the painting gallery of the Vatican is Raphael's last work, "The Transfiguration."

Every one before leaving the city is expected to purchase a few Roman scarfs, also some mosaics, which are here largely manufactured, the material being given out from the Vatican.

While seated at breakfast our *cicerone* informed us that we could see Mastai Ferretti, the Pope. Hastening to the Vatican we left our carriage near the colonnade, then walked up the long marble steps between files of papal soldiers, and took our position at the entrance of the hall. In a moment his Holiness stood in front of us; and reaching forth his hand, with three fingers extended, gave us his blessing. He has a mild and pleasant countenance, his hair is white with the frost of time, and he moves with a slow and steady step. He was dressed in a crimson velvet robe, embroidered with gold, with an ermine tippet, and a black velvet cap upon his head. Accompanied by two of his cardinals, who wore long black velvet robes, and followed by a long train of attendants, he entered a massive carriage, richly decorated with gold ornaments, and drawn by six superb black horses, surrounded by a mounted body guard of about two hundred and fifty. The cortegé moved to the church of the Maggiore. As they passed along the streets many of the people fell upon their knees.

Over sixteen years the Pope has been guarded by French troops, who have recently been withdrawn. As Rome is now to be the capital of Italy, and the residence of its king, we may expect a great change.

Will Rome again become a powerful and a splendid city? Under the new regime, the first element of which is the separation of the Church and State, everything is possible, though the most devotedly blind adherents to the Pope see in his loss of temporal power, the decline of the principle of religion in society; forgetting that superstition is not necessarily piety, nor blind devotion to dogmas a sign of religious sentiment. Certainly this is the age of iconoclasm, but we must expect the first effects of religious freedom to be extravagantly disorderly; still we may trust to nature in this as in all other cases, to establish the equilibrium. Give the railroad, the telegraph, and the public school a fair show against the dogma of Infallibility and the dogma will have to yield. Rome, the capital of free Italy, may yet become the "mistress of the world" in a far nobler sense than ever before.

CHAPTER XIII.

FROM ROME TO NAPLES.

THE Romans enjoy at least one luxury during even the warmest months of the year, they have an abundance of pure cool water. In summer it is not considered prudent for strangers to leave their rooms before sunrise or after sunset owing to a malaria which arises from the Pontine marshes.

These marshes are the low southern portion of the Campagna—a vast tract of land surrounding Rome. The soil of the Campagna is volcanic, some of its lake basins being extinct craters. The marshes cover a plain some twenty four miles long and eight or ten miles wide, being formed by several small streams that flow down the Volscian mountains, and finding no outlet to the sea through the sand drifts, spread over the land. Once, however, the site of the Pontine marshes was dry, for the Appian way was carried over them some three hundred years before Christ. Julius Cæsar, Augustus, and others have attempted to drain them. A canal was dug along the Appian way which Horace in the year 37 B. C. speaks of traveling over. The miasma rising from these marshes is not often carried as far as the city except by strong south winds.

Leaving Rome in the morning we were again subjected to the passport and luggage annoyance, as the Papal authorities are more strict than any which we have found in Europe.

Riding along the Campagna, on every hand are relics of ancient Rome—here an old castle, there an old wall or tower, and for a long distance out of the city can be seen the ruins of the old Roman acqueduct, one of the famous relics of the ancient wealth and greatness of Rome.

The female peasantry are at work in the fields, some gathering while others are preparing vegetables for market; they appear industrious and cheerful. It is a well known assertion that the moral

ITALIAN PEASANTRY.

condition of the country people of Italy is much superior to that of those residing in the cities. We passed large orchards of cork trees, many with the thick bark recently taken off the trunk for exportation. Quite a revenue is derived from this source. One notably picturesque scene attracts our attention as we drew near the city of Naples. This was the peasant women carrying quaint vases of water on their heads.

At Caserta, on the route, is the palace where formerly resided the king of Naples. It is a large and elegant structure, now unoccupied, covering several acres.

Here the vineyards, which are the wealth of Italian husbandry, have a lovely peculiarity. The vines are twined from tree to tree by means of a rope, and hang in beautiful garlands.

"Here the vines wed each her elm."

Rattling through the streets of Naples to the Hotel de Amerique, we are once more in sight of the Mediteranean, with the steamer *Quaker City* anchored in the bay.

Naples is proverbial for the beauty of its situation; it is built along the bay of Naples, forming a half circle or crescent, and like the rest of the Italian cities, it has plenty of churches, priests, and lazzaroni. The Neapolitans are a gay people and devotees to the shrine of pleasure. They think much of their beauty, and the height of their ambition is to ride in a carriage along the fashionable drive by the bay. Women of any social rank do not walk in the streets, it being derogatory to their dignity. On the flat roofs of their houses adorned with shrubs and flowers, the women frequently find nearly all of their out-of-door exercise. Living costs but little to the poor of Naples. Three cents procures a meal of macaroni, and three more a dish of good fish, or vegetables fried in oil. These luxuries are supplied by the itinerant street cooks. For a fraction of a cent the Neapolitan has a glass of iced water, and for two, an addition of sugar and grape juice. Ice is abundant from natural ice caverns in the rocks above Sorrento and even on Vesuvius. This ice is taken out in the evening, and made to slide

NAPLES BAY.

NAPLES WAGON.

down the mountain on ropes ; then it is put into boats which carry it across the bay and land it in the early morning.

The street scenes are very animated. Here and there are groups of girls, not the most tidy looking, some playing upon musical instruments, others singing. Along comes a curious kind of vehicle drawn by one horse. It is a platform set upon two wheels with a high and low seat, filled with people. On the front and back stand those who cannot sit down, the number sometimes ranging from twelve to fifteen, a motley looking crowd, all talking and laughing.

I was exceedingly amused to see the old market men and women trotting along with their donkeys loaded with vegetables, each donkey decked out gaily with different colored worsteds on their heads and strings of large blue beads around their necks. Some with great frames on their backs filled with lemons, figs, grapes, peaches, pears, and apricots.

The fruit here is delicious, plenty, and very cheap, and in the fruit season forms the chief article of food for the people. With this and a little macaroni they make many a meal.

Flower girls are numerous and often annoyingly persistent in selling their bouquets. They seldom ask you to buy, but running along beside your carriage, toss their flowers into it and keep up the chase until they get their pay. If you hand the flowers back they are sure to toss them up to you again, so the most satisfactory way is to purchase at once. Frequently in the evening, the street singers would come beneath our window, and with their clear voices, would sweetly sing their native songs.

This place is a great coral mart. No one should come to Naples without calling into the coral shops to see the exquisite workmanship.

An interesting excursion from the city is to the Bay of Baiae, and the hot mineral springs, formerly called the hot baths of Nero. Cæsar, Augustus, Tiberius, Caligula, and Nero once resorted to this place, which was the fashionable resort of the Roman nobles, who for want of room often built their

NEAPOLITAN FLOWER GIRL.

houses out into the bay. Their submarine foundations are still to be seen, as are also certain circular buildings which they built for their hot baths. To reach these baths we passed through the Grotto di Pozzuoli, a tunnel over 2000 feet long and excavated in the mountain. Near the entrance is the celebrated columbarium covered with vines, called the tomb of Virgil.

The mineral baths are much resorted to by invalids, and the building over them is fitted up conveniently with many bath-rooms. In the center of the reception room is a fountain of hot water, and under the hall the proprietor showed us one of the natural springs. The steam that arose from it was hot and suffocating.

The Neapolitans have two Campo Santos, one where the wealthy are buried with much care, the other for the poor who are all huddled together in one vault. All the funerals take place at night. The explanation given is that the sight of the funerals passing through the streets in the day time had so serious an effect on the minds of the people, as to often produce a panic; and for this reason the government ordered that all burials should take place at midnight. Returning to our hotel one evening, we met one of these funeral processions, and were informed that it was some rich person who had died. There were a number of men walking in white masks and gowns, carrying long lighted candles; following were several priests chanting. The coffin, which was covered with black velvet and gilt trimmings, was costly and elaborate. It was borne on the shoulders of men, followed by the relatives and friends of the deceased.

The castle of St. Elmo crowns a high rock overlooking the whole city and guarding it by its numerous guns.

The figure of the Veiled Christ, in one of the chapels, is a very curious work of art. It is a full length figure over which rests a thin, delicate veil, so gauzy that through it each feature is distinctly visible, and even the expression of the face, and yet it is all wrought out of a solid block of Carrara marble. We did not learn the sculptor's name.

In the cathedral of Naples is the celebrated Chapel of San Gennarro or Saint Januarius, the patron saint of the city. This Chapel contains the two vials of the blood of the Saint—on ordinary days apparently a small quantity of dried substance in the bottom of the vials. Another chapel contains the Saint's head in a glass case. These are exposed to public view on certain occasions, and when the head is brought near the bottles an alleged miracle occurs. The dark substance in the vials is seen to grow red and then rise and bubble—to all appearance becoming fresh blood. This liquid soon falls again when the head is removed, and returns to the original dark dry substance. During the feast of St. Januarius this miracle continues some days, and scientific men have witnessed it and have given more or less plausible explanations of it; but it is needless to say that they would not be permitted to subject it to a scientific investigation. Relics must not be subjected to the touch of sacrilegious hands. Roman Catholics believe the liquefaction of the blood of Saint Januarius to be a real miracle. Pope Pius II. mentions the miracle as early as 1450.

To describe the rich collections of the Museo Borbonico would require too much space. It comprises a vast and ever increasing collection of treasures from the excavations of the buried cities of Herculaneum and Pompeii, besides its galleries of paintings, statuary, Egyptian antiquities, bronzes, pottery, coins, and its valuable library. In several of the galleries artists were busy copying the works of the masters.

In parting for a time from the museums and galleries of art in Europe, I take the liberty of saying that I have often noticed Americans bestowing much unnecessary admiration on works of art, simply because some guide book had extolled them. On the other hand, there is much to be seen which cannot fail to excite wonder and admiration; for instance, I do not understand how any one can gaze upon Murillo's "Conception" in the Louvre, Raphael's "Transfiguration" in the Vatican, Giovane's "Last Judgment," and Tintoretto's "Paradise" in Venice, or Paul Veronese's "Holy Family" in Florence, and not go away deeply impressed with the conviction that they are the human soul's highest conception of divine beauty.

CHAPTER XIV.

VESUVIUS AND POMPEII.

THIS delightful day we have ascended Vesuvius. Reaching Resina our carriage was immediately surrounded by a crowd of forlorn looking Italians all anxious to be employed as guides up the volcano, some with donkeys, others with horses, each one declaring his animal to be the best and safest. After a great deal of confusion we succeeded in selecting our horses and commenced the ascent, the crowd following a long distance until they were driven back. The guides whom we had chosen kept whipping the horses and urging them forward with a peculiar call, which the animals appeared to understand. Gradually rising for nearly five miles our path lay

ERUPTION OF VESUVIUS.

through vineyards until we came to a large open field of lava. Our horses with much difficulty picked their way over this dark and uneven surface, until we reached the Hermitage, which has been built for the convenience of travelers, and at which place the government has built an observatory.

The distance to the cone being not over two miles from here, they can accurately foretell when an eruption is to take place; no one is then allowed to approach the mountain.

Crossing another lava region we reached a sandy plain at the foot of the cone where we leave our horses. Holding fast to a leather strap which was drawn by the guides, we commenced the laborious task of ascending. Several times I began to doubt that I should ever reach the top. The more I toiled the longer seemed the way, for my feet would sink into the scoriæ and slip down the almost perpendicular side. At last by perseverance we gained the summit of Vesuvius. The interior of the cone was quiet and presented a magnificent spectacle. Stepping down upon the crater, which was hardened, we crossed to the center. Through the crevices of the crater would come hot blasts of sulphurous air, for the moment making it difficult to breathe; and often it would sound hollow under our feet as though we were standing upon a thin crust. Here we looked down several hundred feet into the fiery mouth of the volcano. The sides all around are covered with incrustations of sulphur of the most lovely shades of yellow, brown, red, and green. While gazing I began to feel faint, my breath became short, and, with assistance, I hastened back to the outer edge, where I soon revived.

Not many years ago, two travelers exploring Vesuvius, ventured too near the center, when one of them fell a distance of several feet. His companion could hear his voice calling for help, but he could not see him. Procuring a rope he threw it over, but it was too short, as the crater on which the unfortunate man was standing had crumbled under his feet and he had fallen again. His voice could still be heard growing fainter and fainter, until the narrow ledge gave way and he was plunged into the awful gulf. We are told that suicides often occur among the Neapolitans, one of the frequent methods being to ascend Vesuvius in time of eruption and throw themselves into the terrible furnace. But I am digressing.

The sun is setting; the west is suffused with crimson and amber clouds. The city of Naples is plainly seen scattered along the shore of the bay. The island of Capri lifts its rocky head out of the blue sea, and down upon the plain we perceive our group of horses, mere specks upon the sand, awaiting our return. To the east, as far as the eye can reach toward the Adriatic, are Italian villages dotting the landscape. The descent to the plain is a work of but a few minutes, though at every step the feet are buried deep in the ashes. It was long after midnight when we drove into Naples, and greatly exhausted we welcomed rest and sleep.

Entering the silent city of Pompeii, what a lonely scene presents itself as we walk through the deserted streets. All is quiet. Now and then a lizard darts across our path and hides beneath some old stone or ruin.

As we wander along through this silent city, the mind runs back almost eighteen centuries when these streets were thronged with the gay and thoughtless. Yonder amphitheatre was crowded with an eager multitude watching the combat of gladiators. Here in the Forum the statesmen eloquently addressed his fellow-citizens. In that Hall near by the sound of revelry was heard. Around those fountains, and in that temple, walked the proud and envious. In this villa, assembled at the festive board, were a goodly company, making merry with the choicest wines and viands. Here upon these seats a vast concourse of people applauded as the curtain fell, and the actor was called to the front of the stage. In that prison gloomily sat the chained criminals. At the gates of the city were posted the sentinels.

What means this cry of alarm? Whence the wail that sounds through the streets? The heavens are darkening, the moon is turned to blood, the air is thick with falling ashes, the music and the dance are hushed, the play stops, the voice of the speaker ceases, the strong tremble, mothers call in vain for their children, husbands search for their wives, friends look after friends, but the terrible shower continues. Higher and higher rises the flood, until all sounds are hushed, doors, windows, arches, temples, columns, towers, walls, and palaces disappear. Where now is the mighty city Pompeii? Buried for ages in a living grave!

We were received at one of the gates, and piloted through the city by a government guard. We walked up one street and down another; across open courts paved in mosaic; into many of the houses where the walls were covered with frescoes and the halls paved with polished marbles. We are led up and down several flights of stone steps and climb over broken columns. After inspecting the public baths, with marble tubs, we pass out of the Herculaneum gate, where we see the sentinel's box, in which his skeleton was found. Gathering a few sprays of ivy which covered the box, we bid farewell to the deserted city. Returning to the hotel, we began to make preparations to leave Europe for the East, as to-morrow we go on board of the steamer Quaker City.

CHAPTER XV.

THE PILGRIMS.

HERE floats the excursion steamer in the harbor. We cannot mistake her with her bright red wheels and " U. S. M," " Uncle Sam's" monogram, on her sides. From her mast head is floating the stars and stripes. A small boat conveyed us to her, and as we stepped up the gang plank to the vessel's side, I endeavored to realize the fact that this was to be our home for months. We were met by the captain's wife who kindly called the stewardess to show us to our stateroom, No. 29, which we found neatly arranged and more spacious than those of the English steamers. It had two berths, wash-stand, and a long seat with a cover, which you could raise and pack away many articles. This had a cushion covered with red velvet forming a sofa. The state-room also contained a mirror, a number of shelves, and the floor was nicely carpeted. From our room a small passage led to the ladies' saloon in which were several crimson velvet sofas, easy chairs, and a piano. There are two of these saloons, both with the same arrangement, and both having state-rooms along the sides.

A flight of brightly polished steps leads us into the dining saloon with six long tables. At the windows were pretty damask curtains and gilt cornices.

The "Pilgrims" were gradually gathering on board from their wanderings. As most of them had been making extensive purchases in Italy and Switzerland, they came bearing quantities of packages; some with a stock of velvet and kid gloves, others with rolls of silk and sets of cameo and mosaic jewelry. Many had new gold watches from Geneva. Here come two passengers with a boat load of wine. One elderly gentleman whom they called the Major was showing a very costly coral necklace and set of jewelry. A gentleman from Illinois, who went by the appellation of Deacon, was spreading out some copies from the masters which he had purchased in some of the galleries. Several of the ladies were busy examining the quality of their purchases and comparing prices. The captain has just arrived from Rome, and last but not least, came Mark Twain, one of the "Innocents Abroad." A few were preparing letters to be mailed before we leave for the Orient. One gentleman is seated at the table engaged in writing poetry; he is called the poet of the party. We soon began to feel at home. There was no doubting the nationality of the company, and it was pleasant to hear again our native tongue spoken. Floating around the ship are a large number of small boats with articles for sale; one is filled with a variety of straw work, another with fruits, one had pictures for sale, and in one an old man was playing with bagpipes while on the seat in front of him were two dancing dolls which he kept in motion.

Sailing around us in a boat were two beautiful Italian girls playing on guitars and singing. On deck are some Italians singing the Garibaldi song, which has now become very familiar to us. From here we expected to go to Palermo; but owing to the prevalence of cholera there, we decided to sail directly for the Grecian Islands.

It is a glorious day as we sail out of the bay of Naples. Here at one glance is seen the matchless panorama of the city and its surroundings. As night approaches and the sun sinks in the west, we have the full effect of what I had always longed to see, an Italian sunset. It would certainly be a difficult task to describe the magnificent spectacle, but remembering the many glorious sunsets witnessed in my own loved country, I scarcely am willing to believe that any in the world can surpass them. There is one beauty of the evening sky, however, which I think is peculiar to Italy. I observed it specially at Florence. This is a splendid translucent green tinge which harmonizes better than blue with the golden glory of the stars.

Sailing by Stromboli, the reflection of its fire upon the sky was visible far into the hours of night. It was not far from midnight when we sailed through the Straits of Messina with "Scylla on one hand and Charybdis on the other." Perched upon the shore of Sicily, with its hundreds of glancing lights, could be seen in the moonlight the city of Messina. The next morning we glided along close to the rocky shores of Italy. On the right, far off in the dim haze, towered mount Ætna, with its top of everlasting snow, while at its base are perpetually blossoming orange groves and luxuriant vineyards.

CHAPTER XVI.

ATHENS.

FOR two days our ship was sailing on the Ionian sea. Entering the Grecian Archipelago near Cerigo, we soon passed the islands of Siphanto, Spezzia, Serfo, and Hydra. The atmosphere is very clear and objects are discernable at a great distance. These islands have a sterile and rocky appearance. Grecian villages are built along the sides of the hills, and around the islands were sailing numerous fishing boats, with their curious rigged sails. Rounding a point of land we came to anchor in the harbor of Piraeus, the port of Athens, and about five miles from the city, where the King's palace and the Parthenon could be plainly seen from our ship.

On shore were hundreds of Cretan refugees who had been brought here from the island of Crete, to be taken care of by the Grecian government and the charity of different nations. Women and children were slowly moving to and fro among the tents in which they lived, carrying food from one to another, presenting a sorrowful spectacle of suffering, while their brave husbands and fathers were fighting for liberty in their own native island. As our company are about getting ready to go on shore and visit Athens, word is sent out from the authorities of Piraeus that no one will be allowed to land from our vessel until after we have remained in quarantine for nearly two weeks. Here was something of a disappointment, for bright were the anticipations of seeing Athens, the Parthenon, Mars' Hill, and the ruins of ancient Greece. There they are within plain sight and yet we cannot visit them! In vain did our captain urge that we were a pleasure party, with not a person ill on board; but our steamer had come from an Italian port and the fiat had gone forth, so there was nothing we could do but submit.

The Greek boatmen are not at all bashful. They gathered around with various articles for sale, not anxious evidently to quarantine our money. The process of trading between these boatmen and the passengers was quite amusing. They would reach out whatever article was for sale attached to the end of a long pole; and to receive payment they would hand up a small pail of water into which the gold or silver must be dropped, which, after being well shaken, they would take out and put in their pockets, well assured that if there was any plague about the coin it was completely washed off. In this way quite an extensive traffic was carried on. Under cover of night some of our party made a trip to the Parthenon; we afterward learned that they stopped to gather grapes on the way. Early in the morning another party disguised in the Greek costume, set out for a ramble among the ruins of Athens. They did not have time to examine the vineyards, but were seen from our decks hastily returning followed by Greek soldiers. The chase was exciting; a boat bearing the flag of Greece is seen to leave the custom house; at the same moment a boat left our steamer bearing the stars and stripes. Now it was a race on land and water; but the Grecians were defeated, and the venturesome Pilgrims were brought back in safety.

This is a golden day. The classic land of Greece lies bathed in the sunlight. Yonder is the mountain on which a powerful king sat to see upon this bay his conquered fleet destroyed in a single day. There sleeps in peace the battle plain.

> "The mountains looked on Marathon,
> And Marathon looked on the sea;
> And, musing there an hour alone,
> I dreamt that Greece might still be free."

We can see the hill on which Paul stood and preached with such power to the Athenians. We can see the ruins of temples which belonged to a land of learning, art, and song.

It is the unanimous decision that we will not remain here to serve out the quarantine, but leave at once for Constantinople. The decision is quickly acted upon.

Passing more of the Grecian islands, we enter the Dardanelles. At the fortified town of the same name, a "*Pratique*" or health permit for the passengers to land at Constantinople was given to our steamer without delay. The shores are lined with forts and Turkish towns, and back of every village is a row of windmills in motion, grinding grain. In front of some of the dwellings veiled women were seated conversing together.

Entering the sea of Marmora, the next morning at daylight I was on deck to get the first glimpse of Constantinople which was in sight, with its towers and minarets, its tall cypress trees and the dome of the mosque of Saint Sophia, all forming a charming picture. Sweeping around Seraglio point we came to anchor in the mouth of the Golden Horn.

CHAPTER XVII.

CONSTANTINOPLE.

FOR the first time I am in an Oriental city. We are among veiled women, and turbaned men. Now indeed we realize that we are among a foreign people.

On horseback, with Turks leading our horses, we are slowly moving over the roughly paved streets of Stamboul to the bazaars. The air is filled with the unintelligible jargon of the people. Porters are running in every direction carrying enormous loads upon their shoulders.

Venders are crying their wares, dogs are barking and beggars are following us calling *bakshish! bakshish!* We are bewildered with the noise and confusion.

In Constantinople the bazaars are the shopping resort of the Oriental metropolis. They cover an area of many acres, and the streets are enclosed with arched roofs lighted from above. Along these streets are the little Turkish shops, their average size being about eight or ten feet square. These are opened and closed by doors with hinges at the top. In front is a platform on which the merchant sits smoking a *narghille* or drinking coffee, but always ready for a trade. They set a price upon their merchandise, like the women in the *Halles* in Paris, double and sometimes treble their value, often with no expectation of receiving the amount they ask. If you do not choose to purchase and go away they will send, or come after you to take the goods at almost any price. The bazaars are divided into smaller ones. There are those with shoes, embroideries, pipes, fancy goods, and among others the diamond bazaar. In this one the stock of each merchant is spread out in small glass cases which they freely exhibit. In one of these shops we were shown a very valuable article of jewelry containing about two hundred diamonds of unusually large size, being there for repairs, and we were told that it belonged to one of the Sultan's wives.

The bazaars are crowded all day long, this being the favorite trading place of the people of the city.

We stepped into a café and had coffee served in Turkish style. It was handed on a salver in tiny cups and was dark colored and very strong. No milk is used, but it is made remarkably sweet. This is their favorite beverage.

There are not many wheeled vehicles excepting a few curious looking cabs, and all of those which we saw looked as if they were made fifty years ago, We tried one of them, and it broke down three times in going from Stamboul over to Pera, so we finally discarded it for the rest of the journey. The *araba* is a vehicle for ladies of rank and peculiar to the east.

Most of the transportation of merchandise is done by porters, called *hamals*, and the loads which they carry are truly astonishing. Large poles rest upon the shoulders of the *hamals* between which is swung a bale of cotton, a hogshead of sugar, or a heavy piece of marble; and with this weight they will run along from one part of the city to the other, with comparative ease.

The streets are narrow, without sidewalks, poorly paved and abounding with sickly looking dogs. In one small square I counted thirty-three. The Turks in Constantinople, we were told, have a superstitious reverence for these animals; consequently, they will not allow them to be injured.

The city is divided into three parts, called Stamboul, Galata, and Pera. These are connected by a bridge across the Golden Horn; Pera and Galata being on one side, and Stamboul on the other. Pera is the Frank quarter, or residence of all foreigners, and is the best part of the city. On the bridge over the Golden Horn we see a throng constantly crossing both ways. From this bridge ferry-boats are coming and going up the Bosphorus and across to Scutari. The water is alive with small canoes, called *caiques*. These boats are very light and skim along the water with great speed. In the bottom

TURKISH ARABA.

of the boat is placed a soft cushion for seats, and the Turkish people are sailing about in them in all directions.

The *fez*, a red felt cap with a luxuriant black silk tassel, is worn very generally by men and boys. These latter are often bright eyed, interesting little fellows, though some of them acquire the universal habit of smoking at a very early age.

The women look exceedingly strange to me. They are closely veiled with the exception of their eyes, the lower part of the face being completely concealed with the "*yas mak*" or veil. They wear a loose hanging robe, usually of a bright crimson, or yellow color, with immense sleeves, flowing trowsers confined at the ankles, and sandals on their feet, sometimes with yellow kid boots, and sandals over them. The dress of the ladies of rank is exceedingly elaborate with embroideries of gold and silver, and often of precious stones, on the richest and most brilliant fabrics. In the *harem*, the *forbidden*, the women and children's apartment, the trowsers are fastened just below the knee, and, being very long, fall over in ample folds to the carpet. They are of brilliant silks and elaborately embroidered down the outside. Here let me say that the word *harem* is a sacred word to the Mohammedan and has nothing of the meaning attributed to it by foreigners, solely from the fact of polygamy which is condemned in Christian countries. We must not forget, however, that it is sanctioned by the morals and by the religion of the East; and however false, is looked upon by the people with the same respect with which we regard our monogamous system.

There are still some of the Circassian women to be seen, many of them justifying their great fame for beauty.

We find aristocracy here as well as elsewhere. The *Kibars* come riding through the streets generally on horseback with a retinue of servants, one or two running ahead to tell the common people to get out of the way, others following their master carrying his overcoat, umbrella, and packages. Such are the street scenes which are presented to us in Constantinople.

At night all is still except the barking of the dogs, and the cry of " *Yangun var* " fire! fire! Fires are very frequent, one or two almost every night, as the buildings, being built of wood, form an easy prey to the flames.

CHAPTER XVIII.

THE SULTAN AND THE MOSQUE.

WE HAVE seen Abdul Aziz, the monarch of Turkey. There is nothing striking in his appearance. He is of medium height, very dark complexion, black hair, and dull heavy eyes. He wore the red *fez* and a neatly fitting suit of black.

This man's word is the law of the Turkish empire, and woe be to him who incurs his displeasure. His salutations are cold and calculated to intimidate those around him. He has several palaces on the Bosphorus where he spends most of his time. We were shown one of them, very elegantly fitted up, and told that it was built by the Viceroy of Egypt and presented to the Sultan. After some difficulty we obtained a permit to visit the Seraglio. This palace was the residence of the former Sultan, but is

TURKISH BOYS.

not much used by the present one. Entering the Sublime Porte and crossing an open court we found ourselves in a large square surrounded with buildings. Going from one to the other the "*Dalile*" points out the uses of the various buildings. In one is shown the throne room, in another the private apartments of the Sultan where his wives are never allowed to enter. A large building is set apart expressly for the residence of his wives and young children, which is of course called the *harem*; another for his slaves and servants. There is an attempt to imitate in the structure and decorations the palaces of Western Europe, but they fail in richness and in the taste displayed in the embellishing.

The Sultan generally attends service in one of the mosques on Friday, which is the Mohammedan Sabbath.

The Mosque of St. Sophia is the most noted of all the mosques in the city, although in attractiveness it is much inferior to that of Suleiman the Magnificent, or the Mosque of Sultan Achmed.

We were compelled to leave our shoes at the door before entering, as the Mohammedans consider it sacrilegious to walk into their places of worship with boots or shoes on their feet; therefore no one is allowed to go in without conforming to this custom, which recalls forcibly the injunction in the Jewish Scripture: "Take thy shoes from off thy feet, for the place whereon thou standest is holy ground." The *Imam* or Mohammedan priest leads the service, while scattered around upon the floor of the mosque, which is covered with a kind of reed matting, are many of the devout worshipers, all with their faces to the east—toward Mecca. Some are bent forward with their foreheads touching the floor, others are upon their knees with the Koran before them.

The service is silent, and impressive—not a sound save the low chant of the *Imam* which is heard at intervals. At morning, noon and night, they are called to this service by the *muezzin*, who is appointed to go up into the minaret and call out the hour of prayer. In a shrill and mournful voice

MOSQUE OF SULTAN ACHMET, CONSTANTINOPLE.

that can be heard far over the city, he sings out "*Allah akbar*" "*Allah akbar*" &c., "God is great. There is no God, but God, and Mahomet is his prophet. Come to prayer. Prayer is better than work. Prayer is better than sleep." Instantly hundreds leave their shops, or whatever they may be doing, and going to the marble fountains around the mosques, bathe their faces and hands before going into prayer. I was much impressed with their devotedness. The Mohammedans seem to be a poor degraded people, but they are sincere in their religion; and Christians may well learn the lesson of sincerity from them. I saw many who could not leave their place of business at the hour of prayer go through with their devotions in their shops, in sight of the people who were going along the street. Persons would try to attract the attention of the devotee by throwing down gold pieces, but the mussulman would pay no attention to any one until he had finished his devotions. I do not think that business men in Christians countries get down upon their knees and say their prayers in the middle of the day, especially when customers stand ready to buy goods, jingling gold and silver in their hearing.

This afternoon we went to see the Whirling Dervishes, and a whirling it was indeed! everything seemed to whirl the rest of the day. These people are a curious religious sect of Mohammedans. There were no seats for us save upon the matting on the floor. A venerable looking man with a robe wrapped around him came walking slowly in and took his position on a rug in the centre of the mosque. One and then another followed until between twenty and thirty were all formed in a circle within a railing where only the dervishes are admitted. There they assumed a kneeling position with their heads bent forward. At a signal from the Patriarch they all arose and commenced moving with a slow march around the circle keeping time to some doleful music; on their heads they wore high felt hats. Doffing a light drab cloak, revealing a dress of white, they commenced a rotary motion. The white gowns floated out until each Dervish was

MUEZZIN CALLING TO PRAYER.

more the shape of a pyramid than anything else. During this motion their hands are placed on their breast, then on their heads, and when full speed is attained, they were stretched out, the right hand with the palm turned upward, the left turned downward, and their eyes closed. In this position they continued whirling for nearly a half an hour, when throwing their cloaks about them one after another they slowly left the room and the strange service was ended.

CHAPTER XIX.

ON THE BLACK SEA.

BEFORE leaving Constantinople the American minister and his wife and the American consul came on board our steamer. They were much pleased to meet so many of their own country people.

Sailing by the Sultan's palaces and through the beautiful Bosphorus across the Black Sea to explore the battle-fields of the Crimea, Sebastopol with all its ruins lies before us. We all anticipated being delayed by the authorities at Sebastopol before we could land, as we had been informed that very likely they would not permit us to go ashore, at least that our passports would be subjected to a long and careful inspection. How different was our reception! As soon as it was known that an American steamer had arrived, word was sent from

WHIRLING DERVISHES.

the Admiral of the Sebastopol Navy Yard to Captain Duncan, asking if he could be of any service to us; that his navy yard was at our service if our steamer required any repairs; and instead of the passports being subjected to the closest scrutiny, many of us were not asked even to show them.

A number of Russian ladies and gentlemen came on board during our stay. They were sociable and quite gratified to go over the excursion ship.

It was not long before the Quaker City people were on shore. A more perfect picture of desolation can hardly be imagined. Almost every building in Sebastopol bore marks of the terrible struggle between the Allies and the Russians. Heaps of cannon-balls were lying around. On the battle-field of Inkerman and around the Malakoff scarcely one stone is left upon another. Great furrows are still to be seen where the shot and shell ploughed through the earth, and at a short distance from Sebastopol, acres are covered with the tombs of the slain. In one place not far from the Redan, we saw a trench where three thousand French soldiers sleep their last sleep. It brought vividly to our minds the scene of Sir Colin Campbell and the "thin red line" of his Highlanders at Balaklava, the famous charge of the light brigade, the French troops like spectators in an amphitheatre, looking quietly on as the exclamation burst from the lips of their commander, "*C'est un spectacle mais ce n'est pas la guerre!*" Pieces of cannon and shell lie strewn over the ground, and all of the immense fortifications remain in the same shattered condition as when the war closed. I believe it was one of the terms of settlement of the Crimean war that the Russians should not build up these fortifications again. At the head of the harbor of Sebastopol is the village of Inkerman, at the foot of a high hill which is crowned by massive ruins of walls and towers showing the former importance of the town. Numerous artificial caves are made in the flanks of the hill, being hewn from the solid rock. "The rock cut church of Inkerman" is one of the wonders of the place. It is said that the caves were made by the persecuted Arians and occupied subsequent-

ROCK-CUT CHURCH OF INKERMAN.

ly by Christian cenobites. Remains of chapels, altars, and paintings are found in them.

In returning from the Malakoff to the vessel, we came to a little church out of which came a Greek funeral procession, bearing the corpse of a beautiful young woman. The priest walked ahead carrying a lighted lamp and chanting. The body was carried by ten or twelve young ladies, each one assisting in her turn as pall-bearer, as though it was an honor to be permitted to take part in conveying the body to its burial place.

Following promiscuously were the friends and relatives exhibiting deep grief. Flowers were strewn upon the coffin and the face of the corpse was exposed, so that all might see the features as she was borne along towards the little open grave in a lonely valley. After the simple burial service of the Greek church was performed, she was lowered to her final resting place.

How solemn was the scene! Little did the mourners know there were sympathizers with them though from a far distant land.

At Sebastopol the programme of our route was

changed and we steamed up into the northwest corner of the Black Sea to the Russian city of Odessa.

We are informed by the Odessians that the Quaker City is the first American steamer that was ever in their harbor. This city has an industrious appearance; large quantities of grain are shipped from Odessa to various ports of Europe. The streets are wide and paved with white soft stone which produces a fine dust kept in continual circulation, as there is a strong breeze blowing from off the sea. The trees, houses, and people are covered with the dust. We were informed that during the wet season the mud is equally objectionable.

Here we see in the market place, for the first time in our journey, the inhabitants buying and drinking oil, coming with pails and bottles to purchase it. What kind of oil it was we were not anxious to inquire; it was enough to know the people drank it.

On the corners of the streets sitting by small tables are Jewish money changers, beckoning all to come and change their money.

ODESSA, RUSSIA

We rode around the elevated city in a quaint looking carriage called a drosky. It is a low built comical looking vehicle with four small wheels. The horse is fastened to one side of a long pole by which the drosky is drawn. The horse's gear is very odd. Its peculiarity is a lofty bow that arches the horse's neck, and when he is going very rapidly, it gives one the idea that he is trying to jump through a hoop.

RUSSIAN DROSKY.

At the Arsenal and parade ground was a regiment of Russian soldiers drilling. Their uniform is neat and showy. They all wear white caps.

On the promenade there is a fine statue of the Duc de Richelieu—according to tourists and guides the grand nephew of the famous cardinal. Chronologically, a grand nephew is just equivalent to a grandson; and as there have been six generations since the time of the great cardinal, it is useless to call the original of this statue who died in 1822, the grand nephew of Richelieu. The relationship about which tourists dispute is this: The Odessa Duc de Richelieu was the grandson of the grand nephew of the cardinal. The great cardinal's sister had a son who died leaving *his* son the Marshal de Richelieu. This Marshal de Richelieu, who died in 1788, was the *grandfather* of the statue's original, who so distinguished himself in the Turkish war that the Empress Catharine of Russia made him a major general in her service. After the war he went back to France, but returned and was appointed governor of Odessa.

Returning to our steamer we find quite a commotion among the Pilgrims. It has been decided to visit the Emperor and Empress of all the Russias, who are staying at their summer palace at Yalta, on the shore of the Black Sea, about two hundred and sixty miles from here. The preliminaries have been arranged by telegraph, and to-morrow we leave to call upon their Imperial Highnesses.

CHAPTER XX.

VISITING THE EMPEROR OF RUSSIA.

ON the way from Odessa to Yalta, several meetings were held by the gentlemen in the saloon for the purpose of preparing an address to be presented to the Czar; at the same time the ladies were gathered in groups conversing about the coming event.

This morning we dropped anchor at Yalta. The Governor-general conveyed to us a message from the Emperor "that we were welcome, and he would be pleased to receive us the next day at twelve o'clock." Word also came that carriages and horses would be in readiness to convey the party to the palace, which is about two miles from the landing place.

All is astir on board preparing for the great occasion. The porters are overtaxed in getting out the stored away trunks for the passengers, as the most *recherche* wardrobes must be selected. The ladies' purchases through Europe are now brought in requisition. Paris dresses, laces, coiffures and jewelry are to be worn for the first time. At ten and a half o'clock we saw the spacious row boats belonging to the Emperor nearing our ship. How gaily they were decked out with scarlet and black figured cushions and scarlet cloth and fringe hanging over the sides almost touching the water; each boat was rowed by twelve men dressed in white caps and uniform. They approach the vessel's side with extreme caution, owing to a heavy sea which was rolling in. As the boat would rise upon a wave and sink away, one person after another stepped in until it was filled, when another boat would take its place. In this way all were safely landed. We step from the boat on crimson carpeted steps leading up from the water into a picturesque canopied landing. The ladies occupying the carriages, and the gentlemen riding on horseback we formed quite a procession, numbering over sixty persons.

The gates were thrown open to admit us to the palace grounds. A company of mounted Cossacks were drawn up on each side of the gates, and we passed through in military order, escorted by the Grand Duke Michael, brother of the Emperor, who had met us on the way.

At precisely twelve o'clock we formed in front of the palace. The smoothly cut lawn around us was like a velvet carpet, with a profusion of surrounding flowers. Immediately the Emperor and Empress appeared, accompanied by their daughter Marie, and one of their sons, the Grand Duke Serge, followed by a retinue of distinguished persons.

The American Consul who had come with us from Odessa stepped forward and read a short address to his Imperial Highness Alexander II., Czar of Russia, which had been prepared and signed by the passengers. The Emperor replied to it by saying " that he thanked us for the address and was very much pleased to meet us, especially as such friendly relations exist between Russia and the United States." The Empress further replied by saying "that Americans were favorites in Russia, and she hoped her people were the same with Americans."

The Emperor is tall and well-proportioned, with a mild yet firm expression. The impression of the beholder is that he is one born to command. He wore a white cap and a white linen suit, the coat confined with a belt around the waist and ornamented with gilt buttons and elaborate epaulets.

The Empress is of medium height, fair complexion, and although delicate looking she appears young for one of her age. A bright, welcoming smile lit up her face. Her dress was white foulard silk, dotted with blue and richly trimmed with blue satin. She wore a small sleeveless jacket of the same material and trimming, a broad blue sash, and around her neck was a tie made of swiss muslin and valenciennes lace. On her head was a straw hat trimmed with blue velvet and black lace. Her hands were covered with flesh-colored kid-gloves, and she carried a light drab parasol lined with blue silk.

The Grand Duchess was attired in a dress of similar material to that of her mother, only this was more tastefully arranged with blue silk and fringe; a belt of the same material as the dress, fastened by a large rosette, and a straw hat trimmed with blue silk.

The Grand Duke Serge is quite young, and a well-appearing youth. He was dressed in a scarlet blouse and white pants.

Individual introductions followed. Several of the ladies, including myself, had an opportunity of conversing with the Empress. All of the Imperial family speak English very well.

We were escorted through the buildings by the Emperor and Empress, entering a door which was on either side a bower of flowers. Almost all of the apartments were thrown open. The floors were inlaid and polished, and the furniture was curious and costly. The Emperor took special pains to show us the chapel where he and his family worship. It was very handsome, and connected with the main building.

Every effort was made by the Imperial family to welcome us, and really the Pilgrims seemed to act as much at home as though they were accustomed to calling on Emperors every day.

I could not realize that we were being entertained by a ruler of more than seventy-five millions of people, and whose word was the supreme law of the most powerful nation on the globe.

CHAPTER XXI.

OUR STAY AT YALTA.

THE name of the Emperor's palace is Livadia. It is very beautifully situated on the side of a mountain gently sloping toward the Black Sea.

The grounds have been expensively laid out, and near the palace are gardens filled with choice flowers.

The Imperial family generally remain here during the months of July and August. Near by stands the palace of Worrondow, belonging to the crown Prince, who is very wealthy; we were kindly escorted through his residence, which is nearly as elegant as Livadia. An invitation has been tendered us from the Emperor's brother, saying that he would be pleased to see us at Orianda, his palace, which is between one and two miles from where we are. Driving through the grounds, which are delightfully adorned with large groves of trees, gardens, vineyards, fountains and cascades, we arrive at the Palace of the Grand Duke Michael, governor-general of Circassia, who also resides at Yalta with his family during the summer months.

The balcony is filled with handsomely dressed ladies, watching our approach. The Grand Duke and Duchess at once appeared. He is even taller than the Emperor, and stately in his carriage. He wore a uniform of azure cloth with silver decorations. The Grand Duchess is young, has a dark complexion and is quite handsome, lively, and sociable. Her dress consisted of white alapaca *en train*, trimmed profusely with black barb lace, a drab hat, with velvet and feathers of the same color. The Emperor and family arrived here about the same time with our company. The party now dispersed in various directions through the parks and gardens accompanied by the different nobles attached to the Imperial family.

The Grand Duchess showed us her favorite little

dog, which she informed me had been so much admired by Queen Victoria that she had sent one like it to Her Majesty.

The children of the Grand Duke were playing under the trees, with soldiers guarding them. We were told they are never allowed, when out playing to be out of sight of the guard.

At three o'clock we were invited into the palace to "breakfast." In a splendid saloon opening on a veranda our party were soon seated around many polished round tables on which the refreshments were served. The different tables were honored from time to time by the presence of royalty. While his Imperial highness was seated at our table, the conversation turned upon the Ottoman Empire. Mr. G—— made the remark, " that he thought, ere many years would pass away, Russia would become the possessor of the Bosphorus and Dardanelles." A smile played across the countenance of His Highness as he nodded assent and intimated that such a thing was not at all improbable.

The Grand Duchess now appeared at the breakfast

richly attired in purple silk with satin trimmings sometimes walking along the great banqueting room, and sometimes upon the veranda.

The reception being over, the Imperial party took their positions at one end of the long saloon to bid each one of the visitors adieu as we withdrew. Scarcely had we returned to our floating home before bouquets of flowers were sent on board from the Emperor's gardens, to be presented to each lady.

The next day our steamer was put in complete order. The velvet sofas were brought on deck, the saloon was dressed with flowers, and all had a cheerful look.

We were visited by a large number of the Russian nobility, among them Admiral Glassnap, Admiral of the Black Sea navy; Governor General Kotzebue, and his two daughters; the venerable general Todleben of Crimean fame; Baron Sternberg, Count Fostetus, Baron Wrangel, and other distinguished Russian gentlemen and ladies. A collation was served in the saloon, at which speeches were made and congratulations freely interchanged.

In the evening, the Quaker City was illuminated and displayed fireworks in honor of the occasion.

The next day the Admiral invited us on board of the Emperor's yacht *Tiger* which was anchored off the palace.

We were heartily received on board the yacht. Everthing was scrupulously neat and there were many rooms elegantly furnished. In the Czar's private room were the pictures of the Imperial family, including a correct likeness of himself. The company were here entertained with refreshments. The ladies were offered cigarettes, as many of the Russian ladies smoke. It is their custom at entertainments to offer cigarettes to the ladies.

The third day we anticipated a call from the Emperor, but a heavy sea made it difficult for the small boats to go to and fro between the steamer and land and His Imperial Highness did not care to trust himself in them ; so we had to forego the honor.

At eight o'clock in the evening the anchor was lifted, and we sailed by the Czar's palace, which was brilliantly lighted, and amid the booming of cannon, the shooting of rockets, and blue lights illuminating our ship, we bid farewell to a scene which I shall treasure as one of the brightest remembrances of my life.

CHAPTER XXII.

SMYRNA.

AGAIN the prow of our steamer is pointed across the Black sea toward the Bosphorus. This morning I was awakened early, as we were approaching the city of Constantine. Hastening on deck I found but few of the passengers up. I had the opportunity of seeing the sun rise upon the city of Constantinople. Approaching the city from the Bosphorus a much finer view is afforded than from the sea of Marmora.

The sun was just rising and as its golden light touched crescent, minaret, dome, tower, and cypress as with some enchanter's wand, the city was transformed into a vast sea of flashing lights, and the scene was one of matchless and indescribable beauty which well repaid me for my early rising.

Here we are to remain for several days, until we are thoroughly acquainted with the Mohammedan capital.

More bargains are made with the *Osmanlis* for slippers, chibouks, narghilles, turbans, Turkish towels, beads, and a liberal supply of ottar of roses, which of course is warranted to be genuine. Some of the Pilgrims now begin to dress in Oriental style. We sail every day in the *caiques* upon the Bosphorus and the Golden Horn.

Once more on the sea of Marmora; through the Dardanelles where swam

> "Leander who was nightly wont
> To cross thy stream broad Hellespont."

We sail along the coast of Asia Minor in sight of the place where stood the city of ancient Troy, where Trojan and Hector battled for the beautiful Helen. We pass the islands of Tenedos and Mytilene, the latter of which was one of the most powerful of all the Grecian islands, and said to be the birthplace of Sappho. Steaming up the gulf of Smyrna, it was ten

COUNTRY MOSQUE IN ASIA MINOR.

o'clock in the forenoon when we came in sight of the city. With the aid of our glasses we could see on the shore of the gulf long caravans of camels going into the city.

In the harbor lay the United States gunboat Swatara, and as we sailed close along side they saluted our flag and ran up the stars and stripes. At the same time her crew sprang up the shrouds and gave us three cheers. I realized at that moment how dear to me were the stars and stripes, emblem of my own loved country. It was like meeting an old friend in that distant country.

Smyrna is built around the base of a mountain which is crowned by a ruined castle. It is the largest sea port in Asia Minor; the streets are narrow and crowded with people, donkeys, and camels. It has its bazaars and mosques. We are soon on shore and wandering through the city, dodging here and there to escape the caravans which are moving through almost every street, loaded with figs, raisins, and various products of Asia.

In one of the fig packing establishments we saw

over three hundred bushels of figs, ready for packing. In one of the rooms were nearly a hundred people, men, women, and children, packing the figs. The women, even at their work, were closely veiled, excepting their eyes. The proprietor pointed out a Turkish man and woman at work side by side.

MERCHANT OF SMYRNA.

They were husband and wife, and he informed us that although they had been working for him twelve years, he had never seen the face of the woman. Her husband would never allow the veil to be removed in public.

The bazaars are not as large as the ones in Constantinople, but they are well stocked with oriental goods. Heaps of Persian rugs are seen, some of them handsome and valuable. There is a large trade in them here, and they are brought from the interior of the country by the caravans. On every hand are Turks, sitting cross-legged sipping coffee, and smoking the narghille. This smoking and coffee drinking seems to be the most important business in the eastern cities. It is an old saying that "the first four wishes of a Turk are, rest, silence, pipes, and coffee."

Here it is supposed Homer was born, and here also was the residence of the Apostle John. The site of the church of Smyrna, one of the seven churches of Asia, is pointed out. Alas! Ephesus, Smyrna, Pergamos, Thyatira, Sardis, Philadelphia, and Laodicea—thy greatness is with "the dream of things that were."

Some of the country mosques in Asia Minor are

exceedingly beautiful and though small in size are elegant in design and finish. The mosque is everywhere substantially the same in plan, being square and surmounted by a dome. The first mosque, erected at Medina by the prophet himself, has served as a model for all that have been built since, though the minaret seems to have been an afterthought of the time of the Caliph El Walid.

We constantly meet the Pilgrims scattered over the city seated around shops, drinking coffee and lemonade, eating figs and dates, and enjoying themselves generally.

To-morrow we leave for Ephesus.

CHAPTER XXIII.

EPHESUS AND ITS RUINS.

A RAILROAD has been built by an English company, running from Smyrna sixty miles back into the country, for the purpose of bringing into the city the various products of Asia, which are brought to the different stations by caravans. This road runs within three miles of Ephesus. Arrangements have been made with the president of the company to convey our party by special train to Ayasalouk, the nearest station to Ephesus. At five o'clock in the morning we leave the steamer and are soon in the cars. Large droves of camels, horses, and goats were grazing in the fields along the way, and almost every native was armed. It was not unusual to see a man with two pistols, two knives in his belt, and a gun resting across his shoulder.

We were in charge of a tall jet black Nubian, who was heavily armed and dressed in a showy eastern costume. He walked up and down, and gave his orders like one who was invested with high authority, and seemed to look upon us as much inferior to himself.

From Ayasalouk we rode on donkeys to the ruins. Crossing a level tract and over a high hill we descended upon the plain of Ephesus. Nothing is to be seen of that once splendid and powerful city but a vast desolate plain of ruins. The Theatre of Ephesus, where Paul preached, and where Demetrius the silver-smith addressed the multitude, when they all with one accord cried out "great is Diana of the Ephesians," is first inspected. It was built of pure white marble. The seats are almost perfect, although covered with earth. It is in the form of an amphitheatre, and would seat many thousand people. A space two or three feet wide of the earth has recently been removed, revealing from the foundation to the top, a distance of nearly two hundred feet, the white marble seats in perfect preservation.

In the ruins of one of the Temples we saw beautifully carved pillars, thirty to forty feet in length, ten to fifteen feet in diameter, lying broken, their fragments scattered upon the ground, as though some earthquake had hurled them from their foundations.

The best preserved structure is a beautiful mosque, built in the fourteenth century, over the grave of St. John, and on the site of the church of Ephesus. No one could tell us where the Temple of Diana had stood—not a stone to mark the spot.

We gathered in the amphitheatre where it is supposed Paul fought with the wild beasts, and our artist Mr. J——, photographed the scene.

The Aqueduct, which was nine miles in length, could be traced for a long distance by the lofty and massive marble columns on which it rested. History tells us that in the days when these ancient cities were built, oftentimes as much money was expended upon the construction of the aqueducts as it required to build the cities themselves.

The cave of the Seven Sleepers, the tomb of

Mary Magdalen, the hill of Pion were all explored. High upon a rocky hill stood the "Prison of Paul," built of mammoth blocks of gray stone. Climbing up its rugged sides a few of us seated ourselves and listened to the reading of Paul's imprisonment. There spread out upon the vast plain below was all that remained of that once mighty city! Its ships which brought the treasures of the world to its doors are all gone and its harbor is sealed up. The voices of the Ephesians are hushed forever and the only sign of life that we can see amid its ruins, is a lonely shepherd crossing the valley and calling his sheep to follow him. We remained for a long time deeply interested in the picture before us. As we were preparing to descend from the mountain prison, Colonel K—— handed to each one a cup of wine, accompanied with the remark that it was not likely any of us would ever meet there again.

CHAPTER XXIV.

FROM SMYRNA TO SYRIA.

TO-DAY is Sunday, and we listen to a good sermon from the Rev. Mr. B——, one of the excursionists. Every sabbath services are held on our steamer.

Again in the Grecian Archipelago, the islands of Scio, Samos, Patmos, and Rhodes come in sight. On the highest point of the island of Patmos, we can see the convent built over the cave where St. John wrote the Revelations. These islands were once rich and powerful, but since the Turks have ruled them their prosperity has vanished.

Running along by the Isle of Cyprus, we observed many large towns on the hills.

Busy preparations are being made for Syrian travel as we are fast nearing Syria. The company will divide into small parties, some wishing to take one course through the Holy Land, and some another. A few will leave the ship at Beyrout for Damascus, and journey southward from there. A part of the company will land at Mount Carmel, and cross to the sea of Galilee from that point. Others will enter Palestine at Jaffa.

As the weather is very warm, dresses, veils, and hats must be arranged. White prevails as it affords the best protection against the sun's heat.

On the morning of September the tenth, we awoke at Beyrout and saw the sun rising over the mountains of Lebanon. The dawn promised a bright and perfect day. We are to remain here several days to complete the preparations for the inland journey. The American consul and the missionaries are very attentive and very courteous in furnishing needed information and introducing dragomen. Our party numbering eleven here secured a trusty Arab guide. He was a native of Syria, speaking different languages, and was thoroughly conversant with the country. An agreement was drawn up and signed at the Consulate, specifying how many servants, horses, donkeys, and tents were to be furnished, and the price to be paid per day.

While we remain here, the missionaries come out to call upon us, among them is Dr. Thompson, author of the "Land and the Book," who has resided in the East almost fifty years.

The American seminary is located at Beyrout. The scholars were brought to see our ship, which they enjoyed very much. Refreshments were furnished them. They were well behaved and intelligent. The missionary having charge of the scholars informed us that many of the native children make excellent students and learn rapidly.

The young ladies could speak English very accurately. A New Testament, translated into the Arabic language and prettily bound, was presented to each passenger. All the work of printing and binding being executed by native Syrians.

According to the statements made, the missionaries are doing much good, not only at Beyrout, but at the branches on Lebanon, Damascus, and Sidon.

This evening while seated upon deck, as if by magic, the city and surrounding country are illuminated with bonfires, along the shore of the Mediterranean as far as the eye can reach. From every hill-top of Lebanon fires spring up, until night is turned into day. This is called the "Feast of the Cross," and to night it is celebrated by the Maronites. When the "True Cross" was found in Jerusalem by the Princess Helena, mother of Constantine, the news was telegraphed all the way to Constantinople by lighting fires on the hills. This celebration has been continued once a year, from A. D. 330, or thereabout, until the present time.

This morning we visit an Arab school; the master sits in the center of the room, with the scholars around him. They sit upon the floor and each scholar has a large card before him with Arabic characters on it. Every one was talking, creating such confusion and noise that I was glad to retreat. It was the loudest studying I have ever heard. Their severe punishment is the bastinado, inflicted on the soles of the feet. This is a common Mussulman practice.

The climate here in Beyrout is healthy, and fruits are plentiful. The night before sailing for Jaffa

ARAB SCHOOL BOY.

was one long to be remembered. The moon came over Lebanon and cast its silver light upon the smooth waters of the Mediterranean. I lingered long thinking how far I was from my own native land and the loved ones at home.

CHAPTER XXV.

LEBANON.

OMER is ready with the horses at half past six o'clock in the morning. After some delay in selecting such horses as each wishes to ride, we gallop along the streets of Beyrout, out through groves of pines and hedges of prickly pear.

Here we meet a common incident of Syrian travel. A Turk goes leisurely by mounted upon a donkey, his feet swinging and almost touching the ground, smoking meanwhile a long pipe. Some distance in the rear followed his wife on foot, with two children in her arms and a large bundle fastened upon her back. The women do most of the laborious work while the men are idle.

A short distance further we saw "two women

grinding at a mill." The mill was composed of two large stones, one rolling upon the other; one of the women was tending the mill, while her companion was driving the ox. It is probable that not much improvement has been made in these mills since the days of Solomon.

Large orchards of oranges, pomegranates, figs, and dates appear on every side. Crossing the dry bed of the *Wady Kadisha*, we enter a vast plain of olive trees.

At the foot of Lebanon is a manufactory, where a number of Arabs are employed making silk.

The ride up the mountains is difficult, since the path is narrow and rocky. The same day we reached the Convent of Lebanon. This was a Jewish church before the time of Christ, but for several hundred years it has been occupied by Greek monks.

The Convents in the East afford comfortable accommodations for travelers. They are necessary unless the traveler has his own tents and conveniences for camping out when night overtakes him. The old monks cordially received us and soon provided such refreshments as they could. We were in need of rest and felt thankful for their attention.

We are informed that an Egyptian family are residing on the mountain for the summer, near to the convent, and that they are coming to see us. Presently the door opened, and a beautiful Arab lady accompanied by her husband and three little girls entered. She was a brunette, gracefully attired in white with a crimson silk girdle tied at her side; her hair fell loosely about her neck and shoulders, and was adorned with pink and white roses. Her jewels were composed of diamonds and gold. They had come to invite us to their home, and we accepted the cordial invitation. Soon after entering their house, we were asked to sit down, when I found myself instinctively looking for a chair or sofa, forgetting that I was in the East. Our party, now numbering five, were soon seated upon the floor with the family, and servants brought in quick succession figs, grapes, jellies, and pomegranates sprinkled with rose water; then followed coffee. and afterwards for the gentlemen, narghilles, which com-

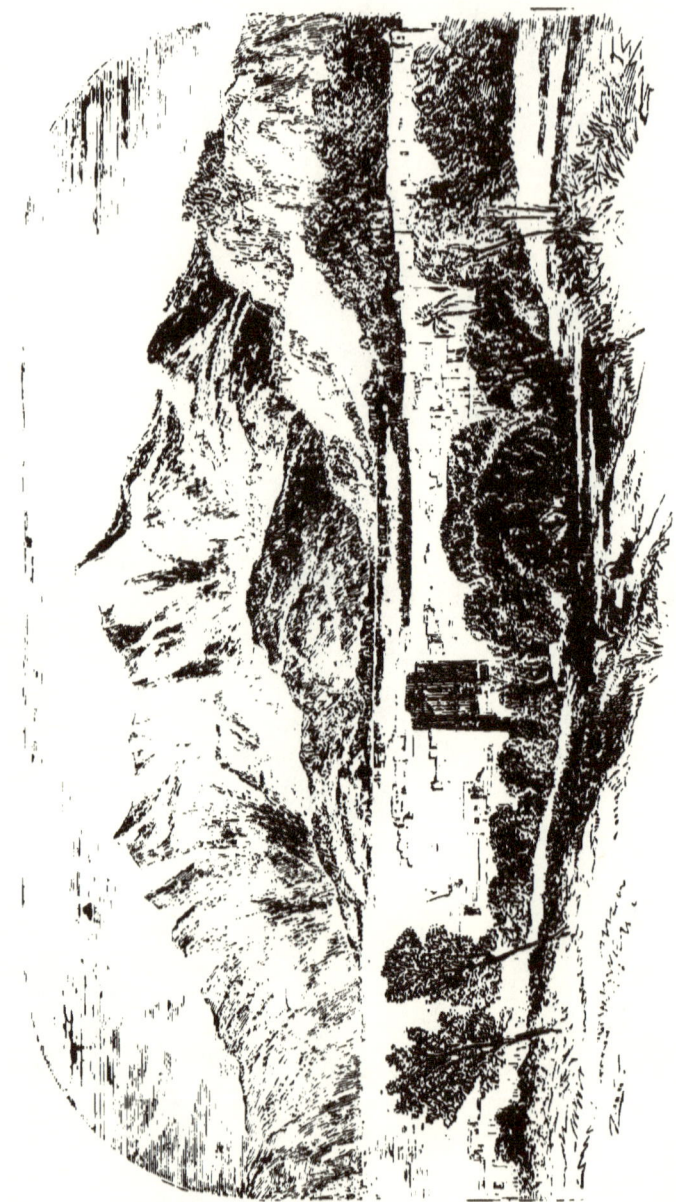

CHAIN OF LEBANON.

pleted the Oriental picture. Through an interpreter, meanwhile, the conversation went forward.

Our hosts were deeply interested in hearing from our country. They wished to know how the people lived and how the houses looked; what kind of fruits and trees grew in America, and whether we had schools and cities; all which information we readily gave them.

The repast being ended, two servants came bearing dishes of water and napkins. One poured the water upon our hands while the other held the basin below.

The lady, our hostess, desired me to go to her apartments. They were furnished with divans, and seating ourselves upon one of them she informed me that her native place was Egypt, but owing to delicate health, she came to the mountains of Lebanon with her family to remain during the heated season. Her little daughters were bright and intelligent. At their mother's request they sang very prettily the hymn commencing "I love Jesus," which they had learned of the missionaries. This performance greatly pleased the mother as well as myself.

She asked me my name, and in return said her's was Mariam, and taking a heavy gold bracelet of Oriental style from her arm she placed it upon mine, saying, "This will make us sisters." At parting she lifted her hand to her forehead and then placing it on her heart bade me an affectionate farewell. We then returned to the convent and mounted our horses. Descending the mountain, for a long time we could look back and see the monks watching us and waving adieu, also Mariam's white dress fluttering in the breeze. We returned to Beyrout by the Damascus road which has been built by the French. On this road a diligence runs daily between the two cities. Damascus, so frequently mentioned in the Bible, is one of the oldest cities in the world, and is still one of the richest of the East. It is the rallying point of all the northern Asia pilgrims to Mecca and the center of Syrian commerce. The population is said to comprise 130,000 Mohammedans, 15,000 Christians, and about 5000 Jews.

Beyrout, or Beirout, is quite a flourishing seaport containing, with the suburbs, about 30,000 people. The modern city was built by Djezzar Pasha. It is situated on a plain behind which rise the mountains of Lebanon. The houses are substantially built of stone, and the flat roofs surrounded by parapets form a very important part. Here, after the heat of the day, the people resort for the cool air, conversation, or the pipe. Sleeping on the house-tops is common in the summer all over the East, the sleepers being protected from the dews by awnings.

CHAPTER XXVI.

JAFFA.

FROM Beyrout our course lies south along the coast of Sidon, now called Saida, and the once splendid city of Tyre, (so graphically described in the twenty-seventh chapter of Ezekiel,) stopping at Haifa at the foot of Mount Carmel. On the summit of the Mount stands the convent of Elijah, built upon the place where Elijah stood when he prayed for rain, and the cloud "no larger than a man's hand" rose out of the Mediterranean. Across the bay we could see the Turkish city of Acre which was once the metropolis of the Latin Christians. Here Napoleon was defeated in the year 1799, and with his defeat he resigned the hope of conquering Syria. Sailing around Cape Carmel the same afternoon, the ruins of ancient Cæsarea came in sight. This city was built by Herod the Great. It is the place where

Paul was imprisoned and brought before Agrippa and Festus to speak in his own defence. His words made such an impression upon Agrippa, that he said to Paul: "almost thou persuadest me to be a Christian." This is the city where so many of the Jewish captives were brought from Jerusalem, and thrown into the amphitheatre to be destroyed by the wild beasts. The place is solitary, and desolate. The fragments of its marble pillars, towers, and walls lie strewn along the shore, half-buried in the sand, or washed by the continual waves of the sea.

The sun is slowly sinking in the west, and remembrances of my Sabbath school days hover around me as I look upon the shores of Palestine. I am about to realize what I had never expected— the sight of the places where Christ and the disciples walked and conversed together, and where the prophets and the patriarchs lived. I am reluctantly compelled to go below to finish packing for the journey, as I shall require thick and thin clothing. Most of the ladies are busy getting ready. The saddles are brought out, for each lady has provided her own, there being no comfortable lady's saddle to be purchased or hired in Syria.

At daylight we are at anchor about two miles off the harbor of Jaffa, with a long procession of Arab boats coming to take passengers and baggage on shore. While tradition tells us that the harbor of Jaffa, is the most ancient in the world, I must say that I think it about the poorest. Josephus describes it as follows: "Now Joppa is not naturally a haven, for it ends in a rough shore where all the rest of it is straight; but the two ends bend towards each other, where there are deep precipices and great stones that jut out into the sea, and where the chains with which Andromeda was bound have left their footsteps which attest to the antiquity of that fable; but the north wind opposes and beats upon the shore and dashes mighty waves against the rocks which receive them and render the haven dangerous."

Our captain informs us that it is not safe for his steamer to lie nearer than about two miles from the shore; and steam is constantly kept up in readiness to run out to sea at any moment should a storm rise.

The usual course of pilgrims visiting the Holy Land is to come from Egypt and land at Jaffa; but whenever there is a storm they cannot go ashore there, but are obliged to disembark at Mount Carmel, or Beyrout. As we neared the shore in the small boat a white line of surf extended along the whole front of the city, but by skillful management our boat was guided over the rocks on a wave and we landed free from harm, although well sprinkled by the spray.

A crowd of Arabs are jostling and crowding to be employed as servants or guides, each one pointing to himself and crying "*bono*" (good), others already asking for *bakshish*.

There is not much to delay us in Jaffa. We see the house of "Simon the Tanner." It is supposed that Noah built his ark here. This was also the harbor where "Hiram, King of Tyre" landed the cedars of Lebanon for the temple, afterward conveying them on camels to Jerusalem.

The "Upper Chamber" is here shown where Peter called the good Tabitha to life.

Jaffa is built upon a hill surrounded by a wall. The dwellings are constructed of stone and are square in form with flat roofs. The streets are narrow and not very clean. The women are strangely dressed. A dark colored cloak is thrown over their heads falling to their feet. A piece of black cloth hangs from beneath their eyes tapering to a point below their chin, or sometimes falling to the knees. This forms a kind of mask and is ornamented with gold coins. Some of the women who do not wear them have their faces tatooed, and wear gold rings fastened through the upper or under lip. They have *khol* about their eyes, and stain their finger nails with *henna*, all of which they consider an addition to their charms.

The only ingress or egress to the city from the land side, is through a fortified gate. Outside of the wall is a large open space filled with natives trading. Caravans are getting ready for Jerusalem, or the desert, and camels are kneeling to receive their burdens.

WOMAN OF JAFFA.

Our first call was upon the Jaffa colony which we found in a poor condition. A few uncompleted houses were clustered together in which the colonists lived. They were heartily sick of the enterprise and wished themselves back to America. It was no place for New England people to settle.

The soil is not very productive, being sandy and the climate warm. How one hundred and thirty Americans could have been induced to leave their homes and go to that place to live, believing they were going to an earthly paradise, is certainly a mystery.

CHAPTER XXVII.

STARTING ON THE PILGRIMAGE.

OUR Dragoman informs us that he is ready for starting. Nijem, for that was his name, is one of the most intelligent of Syrian dragomen, and conversant with various languages. It has been his business for many years to conduct pilgrims through the country. He has therefore become familiar with the history and location of every place of interest.

He is dressed in the full Arab costume, with military belt, sword hanging at his side and gun strapped across his shoulder, presenting quite a war-like appearance.

There have been provided for our company of eleven persons, four tents, fourteen servants or as-

NIJEM, OUR DRAGOMAN.

STARTING ON THE PILGRIMAGE. 227

sistant dragomen, and twenty-six horses and donkeys loaded with the necessary equipage for the journey. This is the form of our agreement with the Dragoman.

Consulate General of the United States of America. Agreement between . . . . of the first part and . . . . dragoman of the other part said . . . . dragoman for the consideration hereinafter mentioned, doth hereby agree:

First: To serve said . . . . as dragoman for a period of . . . . . weeks, beginning . . . . and ending . . . . and for as many additional days or weeks as may be desired by the parties of the first part.

Second: To conduct them from Jaffa through the Holy Land. Visiting successively Ramleh, Jerusalem, Hebron, Bethlehem, Mar Saba, Kedron, Dead Sea, River Jordan, Jericho, Bethany, Bethel, Shiloh, Jacob's well, Nablous, Samaria, and return to Jaffa, stopping at night at convenient and comfortable places.

Third: To furnish tents, bedding, food, riding and baggage animals, saddles, and the necessary services subject to the approval of the parties of the first part. To pay all *bakshish* to guides, sheiks, escorts, servants, and in general, to do every thing which is in my power to minister to the comfort and satisfaction of the parties of the first part, during the continuance of this agreement.

Fourth: In consideration whereof, said parties of the first part hereby agree to pay to the said . . . . dragoman . . . . sterling per day for the period of . . . . weeks, and at the same rate for such additional days as may be hereafter agreed upon.

Fifth: It is understood by both parties, that in case of any failure on the part of said dragoman to furnish every thing required by the foregoing agreement, these may be supplied by said parties of the first part at the expense of said dragoman of the other part, and that any disagreement arising out of a breach of this contract shall be submitted for final settlement to the nearest Consul of the United States.

S. M. G.
B. H. C. } *For the Company.*
G. H.

ﺟﺎﻛﻮﺏ . ﺭﻭﻟﻼ . ﻃﻮﺑﺎ *Dragoman.*

H. E. T.
Acting United States Consul General.

The ladies are privileged to make the first selection of horses. All being ready our caravan starts from Jaffa on our way to Jerusalem, traveling through a forest of fig, orange, pomegranate, and palm trees.

The road is lined with hedges of the cactus plant, full of the red fruit, and here and there we pass a sycamore. The dark foliage of the pomegranate contrasts beautifully with its deep crimson fruit. The orange groves are loaded with delicious fruit, and the air is filled with the perfume of their blossoms. In about half an hour we came to a Saracenic fountain where a number of camels were drinking.

Riding out upon the plains of Sharon, the purple hills of Judea and Benjamin rise before us. The declining sun warns us that night is approaching. In the distance stands the dark Saracenic tower of Ramleh, and hastening on, at twilight we are riding through the streets of Ramleh, the birth-place of Joseph of Arimathea and Nicodemus, and where Christ rested for a short time on his return from Egypt. On the east side just out of the city, we found our camp pitched and every thing made ready for our arrival, as the muleteers and baggage had preceeded us. The Arab cook was preparing our meal over a fire in front of the camp. In one of the tents a table is placed, on which an excellent supper is spread, which is much relished after our fatiguing ride. The ladies' tent was surmounted with a dome, giving it a lofty appearance, while flowers and leaves cut out from red, yellow, and green colored cloths were sewed on the inside, producing a finished and tasty effect. It is carpeted with Persian rugs. Small iron bedsteads stand around in a circle, looking neat and comfortable. This is our first night of camp life in Syria, and we are surprised to see how complete the arrangements are made for the comfort of the Pilgrims. I retired to rest to dream of Jerusalem and Bethlehem which I am soon to see.

CHAPTER XXVIII.

GOING UP TO JERUSALEM.

AT daylight in the morning we are awakened by mournful wailing sounds around our tents. Hastening outside we find that Nijem has pitched the camp near to a Turkish burying place, and there are several women wandering among the graves. They are hired mourners who come every morning at daylight to wail. They are employed for this duty by the friends of the departed. Some of these mourners command a higher price than others. The amount paid them is regulated by their ability to wail and mourn. They wear tear bottles fastened under their eyes in such a manner as to catch the falling tears. They will weep fast or slow as the occasion may require, or the price justify. All this seemed a very foolish and barbarous custom; but when we reflect that the practice of hiring mutes for funerals is still continued in London and in some other Christian communities, we ought to have charity for these ignorant Mohammedans. Dickens and some other English writers have so satirized the custom in England that it is beginning to decline.

It is a clear and balmy morning and we mount our horses and ride over the plain of Arimathea. On the left is ancient Lydda, where Eneas was healed by Peter, and where St. George the patron saint of England was born. We soon pass an Arab town called Jimzu. Here a large number of oxen were treading out grain, which is the eastern mode of threshing.

The heat is intense and I find my white umbrella, hat and veil, affording valuable protection from the sun's rays. At noon we reach the hill country of Judea, but before commencing the ascent of the mountain we rest for a while under a fig tree well filled with fruit. Here Nijem spreads our dinner on a clean white cloth on the ground, around which we remain for some time eating and talking.

Now and then the fresh figs would fall from the tree upon our picnic table.

Near by was a small hut with a roof of old cloth, and bushes under which a number of Arabs were sitting and smoking. They would come and look at us in silence, then go away. After the intense noonday heat was past, we commenced the journey up the bed of *Wady Suleiman* between high rocks, continually meeting camels loaded with heavy burdens, but moving patiently along without turning to the right or left. It was often with difficulty that we could prevent ourselves from being thrown from our horses when meeting these caravans. The second night our camp was pitched in the valley of Adjalon, near to an Arab village supposed to be the Emmaus of the Bible. This has been a restless night; we heard guns fired at short intervals during the night. At two o'clock Mrs. Dr. G—— waked us, and we find the breakfast preparing. Around the fires are seated a number of wild looking men, who had come from the village to demand of Nijem *bakshish* for camping near their town. Each one was armed with a long gun, and had a striped blanket thrown over his shoulders.

We ate our breakfast by candle-light, and the early morning revealed to us Mount Gibeon to the north-east. We are truly on ground made memorable by sacred events. Yonder stood Joshua when he commanded the sun and moon to stand still, while down through this valley swept the Philistines to destruction. We soon cross the stream from which David selected the stone with which he slew Goliah.

After passing a couple of villages situated in deep valleys surrounded with orange and pomegranate trees, we ride over the last mountain, and there before us stood the walls, domes, towers, minarets, and the great dome of the mosque of Omar towering over everything else.

We are in sight of Jerusalem.

CHAPTER XXIX.

THE CITY OF THE GREAT KING.

BELIEVE it is the testimony of almost all pilgrims that they are peculiarly affected at the first sight of the Holy City.

Some years ago when Francis Joseph, Emperor of Austria, approached the city he dismounted and kissed the soil, at the same time remarking that he stood on holy ground.

When the army of the Crusaders, after repeated defeats and long and fatiguing marches, at last came over the mountains in sight of Jerusalem, the whole army as with one voice burst forth into song. I felt that I could remain for hours where I was, before riding within its walls. There stands clear cut against the sky the city which has formed so conspicuous an object in the world's history. It is regarded with affection by the Jews, because David and Solomon reigned there. The Mohammedans call it the "blessed city" for there lived Mahomet and Omar. We love the name of Jerusalem and call it the "Holy City" because in and around it occurred most of the scenes in the life and death of our Savior. It has been taken and retaken many times during the most terrible struggles. It has been conquered by the King of Babylon, Shishak, the king of Egypt, by Antiochus and afterwards by Pompey, Sosius, Herod, Titus, and Omar; consequently it has been occupied by the Egyptians, Assyrians, Jews, Romans, Persians, Christians and Mohammedans. During the siege of the Romans when Titus almost destroyed the city, there perished one million; and one hundred thousand besides these the Romans carried away to Rome, and Ceserea ninety seven thousand captives, it is said, who were thrown into the amphitheatre and destroyed by wild beasts, making nearly one million and a quarter slain by that one war. Later, when the Crusaders under Godfrey De Bouillon took Jerusalem, almost eighty thousand Moslems were slain in and around the Mosque of Omar. When we think that the meaning of the word Jerusalem is "the habitation of peace," the name seems singularly inappropriate.

I cannot realize that I am looking upon the city where all this has transpired. Nijem has hurried on beyond the great Russian convent and we find our camp pitched on the north side of the city, just outside the wall, midway between the Damascus and Jaffa gates.

Jerusalem is built upon a high hill, or mountain with deep valleys all around it, excepting on the north side. It is surrounded by a high and strong wall in which are five gates, four of which are now used. The Damascus gate on the north side; St. Stephens on the east; and on the west the Jaffa gate; the southern or Zion gate is on the south side.

All of these gates are thrown open in the morning and closed at night. Each one is guarded by Moslem soldiers who compel us to hand to them

A TURKISH HOUSE IN JERUSALEM.

every parcel, and if it contains anything of value, a duty is required.

The city is about three-quarters of a mile in width by one and three-quarters in length. It is bounded by the valleys of Kedron and Jehoshaphat, and the Mount of Olives, village and pool of Siloam, Valley of Hinnom, Potter's field, Hill of Evil Council, and the Valley of Gihon. The country around has a barren and rocky appearance, with here and there clusters of ancient looking olive trees. Along the road leading to the gates are Arab women carrying baskets on their heads, filled with chickens, eggs, and grapes. Camels and donkeys are bearing heavy loads in and out of the city. By the road side sit miserable looking *fellaheen* asking alms, while among them are the Lepers.

CHAPTER XXX.

WITHIN THE HOLY CITY.

FEELING much fatigued after my journey, we enter by the Damascus gate and stop at the Damascus Hotel; there are only two here, the Damascus and the Mediterranean. Up a narrow flight of stairs into an open court or stone paved hall, we are shown into a large square room with cemented floor, furnished plainly, but in European style. The walls are high, with niches in them, and there is one double window iron barred. The apartment is not very cheerful looking, but we shall soon become accustomed to it as we are to remain here several days.

This is a calm and bright morning as we go out to explore the city. The streets are narrow and filled with Jews, Arabs, Turks, Armenians, Copts, Syrians, and Greeks. The houses are massive and gloomy, often arching across the street. They are square, and generally have domes on the top for the purpose of keeping the upper rooms cool. Under the houses are large stone cisterns which hold the water, as it rains here only during three months of the year. The water which we used at the hotel had been in the cistern six months, yet it was cool and sweet. Along the streets are Turkish shops, and there is a large bazaar where considerable trading is carried on. Quite a business is done in making and selling curiosities from the olive wood— paper cutters, beads, rulers, canes, boxes, and cups made of it, are offered in almost every street.

We first visit the church of the Holy Sepulchre. Walking under an archway into a large open court we are before one of the most ancient Christian structures in the world. It is an immense building, divided into several chapels, owned and used for worship by the Greeks, Armenians, Latins, Syrians, and Copts, as they cannot agree to worship together. The church is filled with crowds of people, priests, beggars, and pilgrims from many distant lands. Inside of the entrance is a smooth stone slab; this is pointed out by our guide as being the stone on which the body of Christ was prepared for the sepulchre. Turning to the left, the place is marked where the Marys stood to witness the crucifixion. Going through the Greek chapel, which is the richest of all the chapels, up a winding stairway, we stand upon a large rock, said to be the top of Mount Calvary. Here is an altar very tastefully arranged with flowers and lights, and over the altar hangs a very beautiful picture of the Virgin Mary and child, with an inscription formed with diamonds.

Returning to the body of the church, we find the different worshipers thronging toward the sepulchre.

While they cannot agree to worship in the same room, they are willing to go through with their devotions under one roof, and I noticed that once during the ceremonies they all visited the tomb of Christ. What a beautiful thought, that whatever our differences may be, we can all meet around the tomb of the Savior.

HOLY SEPULCHRE.

Under the dome is a small chapel supported by sixteen marble columns. The first room is six by ten feet. Here is the stone on which the angel sat that announced the glad tidings of the resurrection. From there we passed into the inner chamber, or holy sepulchre. It is about six feet square. On one side is a heavy stone sarcophagus, three feet in height. In this the body of Christ lay. The tomb is covered with a white marble slab, and over it hang forty solid gold and silver lamps, which have been kept burning night and day for hundreds of years. At one end stands a monk chanting and sprinkling perfumed water over the tomb. Here Christ burst the bonds of death and came forth to redeem a lost and sinful world. To this spot the nobility of all nations have come to bathe its cold stone with their tears, and I could not but feel the power and truth of the story of the christian religion. Some travelers have disputed about the location of the tomb of Christ, placing it a few feet this way or that. It made but little difference with my feelings; I knew I was standing near the place where my Savior died, and was buried.

The half hour spent here has more than rewarded me for all the trouble of my pilgrimage.

HOUSETOPS OF BEYROUT.

CHAPTER XXXI.

THE PEOPLE OF JERUSALEM.

THE principal occupation of the people appears to be worshiping and performing some ceremony in a church, tomb, mosque, or convent.

The first thing I remember seeing when approaching the city was a procession of nuns, dressed in white, marching from the Jaffa gate down into the valley of Gihon.

Every religious sect in Europe, and the East, apparently, take pride in being represented by a place of worship. A great amount of money is sent here for that purpose. The French catholics have recently bought a site near Pilate's house, and they are erecting an expensive building to be used as a catholic school.

The Armenians have a convent covering a large space of ground. It will accommodate three thousand pilgrims. The church within the convent is finished in mosaic, and contains the tomb of St. James.

The Russian church, which is the Greek, has recently erected a convent on the north side of the city, outside of the wall, covering several acres, and costing an immense amount of money. All this, together with pilgrims continually coming bring quite a revenue to the Holy City.

The protestant religion has the smallest representation here of all the religious sects. There is but one small chapel, which is denominated Christ Church, and supported by a London society. There are one or two protestant missionaries usually residing here, one of whom called upon us at the hotel.

From St. Stephen's gate, where stood the Tower of Antonio, is a street named the Via Dolorosa, leading up to mount Calvary and the church of the Holy Sepulchre. This is the way Christ was led to crucifixion. It passes Pilate's house, *Ecce Homo* Arch, on which the Redeemer stood with Pilate when the people cried out "Crucify Him! Crucify Him!" and the Judgment Hall, which is now used for Turkish barracks.

Priests, monks, and nuns are constantly walking up and down the Via Dolorosa, chanting prayers. Just outside of the north wall of the temple area, is the Pool of Bethesda. It is a large excavation, containing a pool of stagnant water.

There are over two hundred Lepers still in Jerusalem. They live in wretched huts grouped in the south part of the city, called the Lepers' Quarters. They are allowed to marry among themselves, and sit along the highways and beg of the passers by, but are forbidden to have any further intercourse with the people.

The town house of Caiphas, where Christ was confined the night before the crucifixion, and the tower of Hippicus built by Herod the Great, still retain their former massiveness, but show signs of great antiquity. From the top of the Tower of

Hippicus a gun is fired morning and evening, which is a signal for opening and closing the gates of the city. Near by are the tombs of David and Solomon. Over them is a Turkish mosque, containing the "Upper Room" where the Last Supper was eaten, and where the disciples were gathered on the day of Pentecost.

All day long, old Jews and Jewesses are wandering about these tombs. We are told that for over six hundred years no Jew or Christian has ever been allowed to enter the tombs of these great kings, excepting in one instance, about thirty years ago, when a Jew banker of London, and his wife, were permitted by the sultan to descend, and look through a grating, to see the tombs of David and Solomon, for which privilege the banker paid a large sum of money.

One of the most touching scenes which I have witnessed here is the wailing of the Jews, at the "Jews' Wailing Place." It is outside of the west wall of the temple area. They believe this wall has never been destroyed, but is the identical one which

Solomon built. It is composed of enormous blocks of stone, showing the Jewish bevel, which attests its antiquity. As the Jews are not allowed to enter the temple enclosure, they come here to wail. Going there one afternoon, we found nearly a hundred Jews, some on their knees, others bent forward, with books before them, wailing for the loss of their temple, city, and kingdom. The stones are worn smooth with their kisses. They come from all parts of the world to their revered city, to lay their bones near their great ancestors. The proprietor of the Damascus hotel informed us that within the last three years several thousand Jews have come to Jerusalem. They believe that the final judgment of the world will take place here. When we returned to the sea coast we met a large company of old Jews going up to Jerusalem to die.

On the west side of the city, across the valley of Gihon, stands a structure capable of accomodating hundreds of persons. This is called the Jews' Hospital, and has been erected by wealthy Israelites in Europe. If these people who live here have property of value the authorities take it from them, and as they are always idle they have no visible means of support, and whatever they have of value they secrete. It is thought that the Jews know of immense treasures hid in the caves under Jerusalem, from which many of them derive their support. Their history has been one of sorrow and suffering in the East since they were conquered by the Romans. During the reign of Adrian they were driven from Palestine altogether. Under the rule of Constantine they were allowed to come on to the mountains about Jerusalem, and look into the city; but if a Jew was found within its walls he was instantly put to death. Truly, they have been scattered over the earth, and their holy house despoiled.

CHAPTER XXXII.

THE TEMPLE.

NEARLY one quarter of the space within the walls of Jerusalem is occupied by the Temple Area.

It is only within a few years that any but Mohammedans have been permitted to enter the enclosure. We had to wait two days before we could get a *firman*, or written permission to visit it. We were charged for the permit a sum of money, and were accompanied by a mussulman guard, who faithfully watched to see that we did not pollute the place by touching with our fingers anything inside the walls. Excepting Mecca, this is the most sacred place on the earth to the Mohammedans.

In the center of the inclosure stands the Mosque of Omar crowned with a lofty dome, which is the most conspicuous object, seen from any direction in which you approach the city. The mosque stands upon the top of Mount Moriah. Here is the threshing floor, which was purchased by David for fifty shekels of silver, also the Holy of Holies of Solomon's Temple. The interior of the mosque is most elegant, and around the sides are written selections from the Koran.

In the center is a rock called *Es Sukhrah*, on which it is supposed Abraham offered up his son Isaac. It is surrounded by a high railing. Descending several stone steps we come to a cave directly under the rock. For the purpose of entering this cave once the devoted followers of Mahomet will come thousands of miles, for there they stand where their great prophet once stood. They say that the night after his flight from Mecca to Jerusalem he rested in this cave. They also believe that the prayers which they offer up here will surely be answered. Near the Mosque is a marble fountain, at which one of our company stopped to drink, when instantly one of the Moslem

INTERIOR OF THE MOSQUE OMAR.

soldiers sprang forward with drawn cutlass as if to strike down the christian who would dare commit such a sacrilege in the holy place.

In the southern part of the Area stands another massive building called the mosque of *El Aksa.* This is very ancient looking. Some of the foundation of this mosque, is without doubt built from the ruins of the Temple. Here is an entrance to a subterranean passage-way. Going down several steps we came to a vaulted chamber supported by arches and keystones, evidently of great age. The blocks of stone are of wonderous size and probably date back to the time of Solomon. This may have been one of the passages of the Temple. Explorations are going forward by the French and English, and if funds can be supplied, there is no doubt that much more of the plan of ancient Jerusalem and the Temple will be revealed.

Returning to the mosque of *El Aksa* we observed the curiously carved pulpit from which Mahomet preached. Adjoining are two smoothly polished pillars standing over thirty feet in height. The

Mohammedans assured us that Mahomet once passed between them, and all who follow his example will loose their sins. For this purpose the Moslems will undergo a long pilgrimage, and untold deprivations. The pillars stand near together, making it difficult for any one to go between them. Of course we were anxious to be rid of our sins, and consequently made some exertions to accomplish the feat. We all passed between the columns, save the venerable Major, who is quite portly. He made several attempts, being assisted by the Pilgrims, and at one time he became so wedged in between the pillars that considerable anxiety was felt for his safety. He was finally extricated and gave up the effort in despair. It was a favorite pleasantry, for some time after, that the Major was the only sinner left of the company.

Not far from this mosque are to be seen the remnants of the bridge which led from the Temple to Mount Zion, on which Solomon walked with the august Queen who was visiting him, and who exclaimed as he pointed out to her the glory and splendor of his holy habitation, "The half had not been told."

CHAPTER XXXIII.

THE TURKISH FAMILY.

LAST night I was aroused from my slumber by an Oriental marriage procession passing beneath my window. The bride was being borne to the house of the groom, amid the shouts and songs of her friends.

The marriages are generally contracted by the parents of the bride and groom. If the parties are wealthy a large sum of money is paid to the parents of the bride by the groom, which is invested in costly jewels to be worn by her. These become absolutely her property, and thus remain through her life. The jewels can never be taken by law to pay the husband's debts, neither has he the power to dispose of them.

When the day arrives for the wedding ceremony,

or *Nikeah*, to take place, the invited guests assemble at the residence of the bride who is dressed in white and brought out of her home. Sometimes she is seated upon a platform which is carried upon the shoulders of her friends amid great rejoicing, through the streets to the house of the groom where she is met by him at the door and led into the Harem, when the veil is removed from her face, and often this is the first time he beholds the face of his wife.

In company with our hostess to-day, I have visited a wealthy Turkish family. We went on horseback, Mrs. T——, riding her own white Arabian pony. As our horses hoofs rattle over the rough cobble stone pavement of the streets of Jerusalem, it is necessary for us to hold the animals with a tight rein to prevent them from stumbling; for in many places the stones are worn quite smooth. The servant had gone in advance to announce our coming.

We were met by the ladies of the house, at the door of the Harem, where three pairs of sandals inlaid with pearl were standing.

There was no particular ceremony of introduction, further than the information that I was a lady from America. This is Oriental etiquette. The ladies were dressed in flowing robes, silk girdles, full trowsers, and fancy turbans.

We were ushered into the ladies private apartments, the floor of which was white cement, polished to shine like marble. The windows were incased in fine lattices, in such a manner that the inmate cannot be seen while the passer-by is fully visible. On three sides of the room were divans covered with pink silk and lace. Being seated, a Nubian woman brought Sherbet—a kind of lemonade—flavored with rose; after this, coffee in small china cups set in *zerfs*, or stands of gold which were exquisite.

> "And Mocha's berry, from Arabia, pure,
> In small fine china cups, came in at last;
> Gold cups of filigree, made to secure
> The hand from burning, underneath them placed."

Then followed cigarettes, which the ladies folded dextrously.

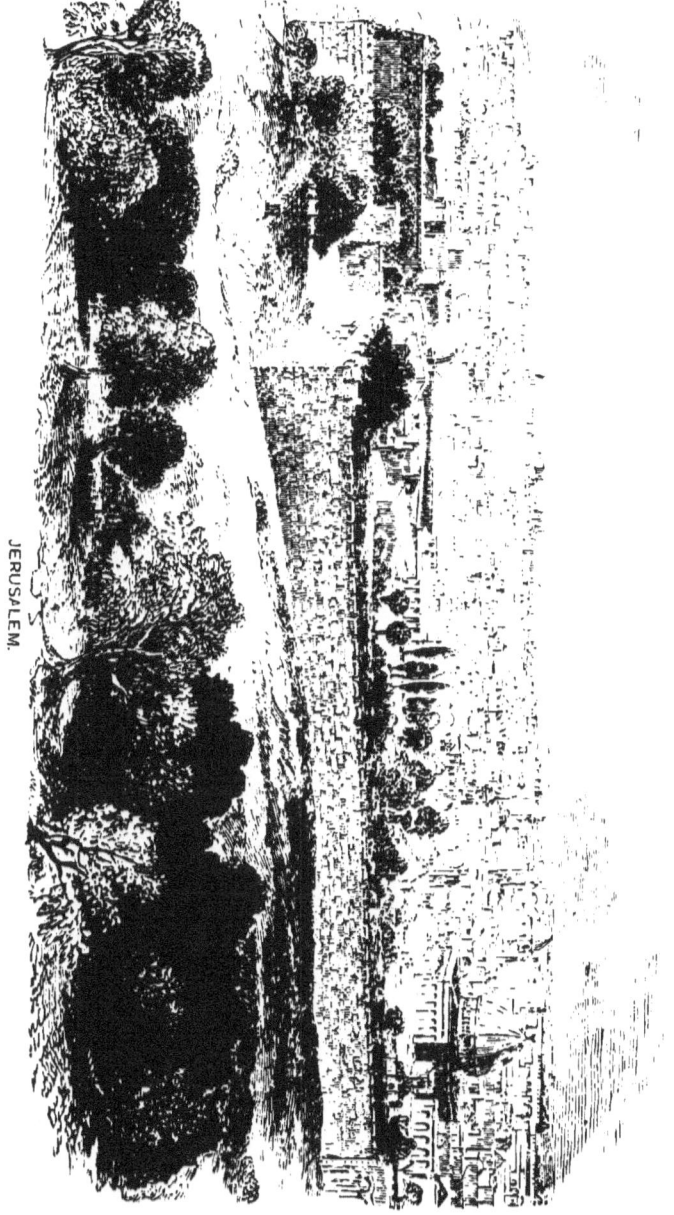
JERUSALEM.

It pleased them exceedingly when I informed them that although I did not smoke, I would take the cigarettes home with me as a souvenir of the pleasant visit. Upon this they wrapped them in white silk and presented them.

The inspection of my garments was next in order. These they examined thoroughly, even to the buttons on my dress, and were much interested in trying on my gloves. They then brought forth their wardrobe of rich silk gauze and Persian stuffs, embroidered with gold tinsel. They wished to robe me in them, but I had them bestow the compliment upon my friend Mrs. T——. They showed us through the rooms of the establishment and also took us on the top of the house, which had a stone parapet six or seven feet high running around the the edge. Through this wall were holes to enable the women to look through.

They were unremitting in their attention. After the ceremony of leave taking, which is simlar to the meeting, we bade them good-by.

One of the characteristics of the East is hospitality, and there is no lack of social politeness.

We returned by the way of the Bazaar.

CHAPTER XXXIV.

OUTSIDE THE WALLS.

ON making the circuit of Jerusalem outside the walls, we start from the Damascus gate toward the east. Going a distance of eight or ten rods, we come to the entrance of the caves under the city, whose existence had been unknown to the world for many centuries, until some years since a missionary in making explorations around the city discovered them by means of his dog. Having procured our guide and torches we crept upon our hands and knees through a small opening under the walls, and gradually descending over two hundred feet, we find ourselves in a room of great height and width, chiseled out of the rock. Pursuing a downward course, presently we come to another cave still larger. Here are huge blocks of stone lying upon the ground, others in the sides hewn and almost ready to fall, just as the workmen left them, thousands of years ago. It is thought that here Solomon obtained much of the material for the building of the Temple; a belief which has been much strengthened by the recent discovery of a passage leading down from the temple area to the caves below. Probably, during the terrible sieges of Jerusalem in ancient times, the women and children have found a refuge in these subterranean vaults. Another theory of historians is, that immense treasures have been secreted by the early nations in these vast caves. In one stands a large pool of water, into which we throw a stone and hear the hollow echo reverberating through the dismal chambers for many seconds. We find the place damp and disagreeable, and we are glad to return to the sunlight and fresh air.

To the northeast of the city are the tombs where were buried the Jewish Sanhedrim and the ancient Kings. The Sanhedrim was the highest judicial and legislative body of the Jews. It was composed of seventy members, and they met daily, with the exception of Saturday, in the "hewn stone chamber" of the Temple. Napoleon I. convened a sanhedrim of seventy-one members in 1807 in Paris, for the purpose of regulating Jewish affairs in France.

With lighted tapers we explored these empty vaults and receptacles for the dead. Silence and darkness prevailed.

Turning around the northeast corner of the wall and going southward, we reach St. Stephen's gate, from which a rocky path leads down into the valley of Jehoshaphat and across the brook Kedron to the Garden of Gethsemane. It is surrounded by a high stone wall. Knocking at an iron door, the only entrance, we are received by a Latin monk, who guides us around the garden. Within the enclosure are beds of flowers and several ancient olive trees.

It was here that our Savior was betrayed and spent the hours of agony. I could not gaze upon the spot

"Without high thoughts and solemn, of that scene
When, in the Garden, the Redeemer prayed—
When pale stars looked upon his fainting head."

The monk gave me a bouquet of flowers, which he had plucked in the garden. I shall press, and treasure them, as one of the most valuable souvenirs of my journeyings.

Close by is another walled inclosure, to mark the place where the disciples slept. A short distance to the north is a low flat stone building. We cross an open court and go down thirty to forty steps, and are in the Tomb of the Virgin Mary. Different colored lights are suspended from the ceiling, and the interior is filled with clouds of burning incense. A long procession of priests, monks, and nuns are marching to and fro, with lighted candles. Mingling with the throng we are soon beside the tomb, which is at one end of the cave. It is of white marble, and over it are strewn white roses. We are told that once a week this service takes place, to commemorate the hour Christ died upon the cross.

Following the dry bed of the Kedron, down the

valley, on the left we come to the Tombs of Jehoshaphat, Zechariah, and the Pillar of Absalom, all cut in the rock. This was the King's dale, and here Absalom erected this monument. A noticeable peculiarity is, that it is almost covered up with small pieces of stone thrown by the Jews. They have a custom of tossing a stone at it every time they pass, which is for the purpose of showing their contempt for Absalom's conduct toward his father David.

We are now in the valley of Kedron. Turning to the right, by the village of Siloam, we stop to bathe our faces and drink of the clear, cool water of the Pool of Siloam. The maidens of Jerusalem are carrying the water from the spring in earthen jars upon their heads up to the city. It is indeed an ancient picture.

To the west of the pool and south of the city, we cross the valley of Gehenna, or Hinnom. Here stood the statue of Moloch, into whose fiery furnace were cast the victims amid the shouts of its worshipers. God being displeased with their conduct, the prophet Jeremiah pronounced a curse upon the ground, saying, "It shall no more be called Tophet, or the Valley of the Son of Hinnom, but the Valley of Slaughter, for they shall bury in Tophet till there be no place." During the Roman seige this prophecy was fulfilled by the burying in this valley of over one hundred thousand of the slain, until there was no more room. Here a fire was continually kept burning to consume the refuse cast out from Jerusalem. No doubt Christ used as an illustration this valley, "Where the worm dieth not and the fire is not quenched."

To the Southeast stands Potter's Field, the burying place for strangers, and the Hill of Evil Council, on which the Jews formed their conspiracy against the Savior. The path leads around the base of Mount Zion to the Valley of Gihon. In this valley on the west side of the city is the Pool of Gihon, where Solomon was crowned king over Israel, in place of his father David.

CHAPTER XXXV.

MOUNT OF OLIVES AND BETHANY.

THIS day is no exception to all the days of our stay in Jerusalem, being extremely pleasant and the atmosphere unusually transparent.

Leaving the city through St. Stephen's gate our horses slowly pick their way along the rocky path across the valley of Jehoshaphat, over the Kedron bridge, and by the garden of Gethsemane, up the side of the mount of Olives, which is still dotted with olive trees.

The olive is the most numerous of all the trees in Palestine and a most useful one to the inhabitants, who derive from it both light and food. It somewhat resembles the willow and bears a small green fruit, which, as it ripens, becomes a purple color. This fruit is largely manufactured in the east into oil, which forms an important part of the sustenance of the people. Extensive orchards of these trees are to be found everywhere scattered through Syria.

Reaching the summit of Olivet one of the finest panoramas in the Holy Land is before us. To the east are the mountains of Moab, the valley of the Jordan and the Dead Sea. To the north are the hills of Benjamin, and in the south Judea's lofty mountains are in view.

Jerusalem lies at our feet on the west. Most of the sketches of Jerusalem are taken from this point. One cannot wonder that Jesus often resorted hither. Looking down upon the city how deep and tender must have been His feelings when He predicted the destruction of Jerusalem, " O, Jerusalem! Jerusalem! how often would I have gathered thy children together, even as a hen gathereth her chickens under her wings, and ye would not!" Here Christ for-told the last Judgment, and preached with such power to his disciples.

The church of the Ascension, now a Turkish Mosque, crowns the hill. We are received at the door, and led to the place where tradition places Christ's ascension, though the Bible leads us to believe that it was further east, toward Bethany.

Here David stood and wept over Jerusalem as he fled to the east of the Jordan crying, "O, Absolom! my son! my son!"

Taking the road which leads around the southern crest of Olivet we continue our journey to Bethany; every place around us has been made sacred by the Savior. Along this path he rode in triumph while the people threw down palm branches before him. Across the valley to the south is the village where he sent the young man to untie the colt. Where our footsteps are treading frequently walked Martha, Mary, and Lazarus, going and returning from Jerusalem.

In less than an hour we reach Bethany situated on the Eastern slope of the Mount of Olives. It is now a desolate looking place, and a few low miserable huts inhabited by Arabs is all that remains of the once beautiful village, where Mary and Martha lived, and where Lazarus was raised from the dead. The ruins of a stone building are pointed out to us as being the very house of Mary. In the rear of a court attached to this house is a monk with a large key. Beckoning us to come where he stood, he unlocked an iron door and we follow him down twenty-six stone steps to the tomb of Lazarus. It is a dark and damp place. An excavation in a heavy block of stone on one side of the cave is said to be where the body of Lazarus lay.

I may here remark that there is more or less skepticism among travelers regarding the identity of many of the places pointed out in Palestine.

There are some good reasons for these doubts, and yet when I behold how solid and enduring are all the structures which are composed entirely of rock and cement, I am inclined to believe that much is still remaining as it stood eighteen centuries ago. It is enough for me to know that I am walking upon the ground and looking upon the identical hills and valleys that Christ and his Disciples looked upon.

Words cannot image forth the fervent emotions and impressions made upon my heart by these scenes.

CHAPTER XXXVI.

BETHLELEM.

IJEM guides us across the plain of Rephaim to the convent of Mar Elias. In one hour we halt by a square stone building crowned with a small dome, inside of which is the tomb of Rachel. " And Rachel died, and was buried in the way to Ephrath, which is Bethlehem, and Jacob set a pillar upon her grave, that is the pillar of Rachel's grave unto this day." We lingered by the tomb of the lovely Rachel. Why was she buried in this lonely place, and not with her kindred at Hebron? Bethlehem is now in sight, with the church of the Nativity distinctly visible. We enter the city through a heavy stone archway, and thread our way toward the spot where Christ was born, followed by a crowd of half-grown Arab boys and girls. Hitching our horses we are invited into

BETHLEHEM.

the convent attached to the church where "raki and jelly" are offered us. After this a Franciscan monk appeared with a large bunch of keys to conduct us through the buildings. We are now in the oldest Christian church in the world, built by Helena the mother of Constantine. Through the Basilica of Helena, and the Greek chapel, we descend several steps behind the altar, and reach the Sacred Grotto or birth-place of the Redeemer. In the marble pavement is placed a large silver star to mark the spot. Around it is this inscription: "*Hic de Virgine Maria Jesus Christus natus est.*" "Here Jesus Christ was born of the Virgin Mary." On the opposite side of the grotto is a marble manger where the original one stood. Most of the people approach upon their knees and kiss the silver star. Among them is our Dragoman, who thus reveals to us for the first time the fact that he is not a follower of Mahomet. As with the Holy Sepulchre, lamps of gold and silver are hanging, in which lights are continually burning night and day.

Here was the stable where Joseph and Mary lodged, "there being no room in the inn." They had come to Bethlehem at a time when it was over crowded with the people, whom the Emperor had summoned there to pay their taxes. In this humble place the Child Jesus was born, who was to live but thirty-three years, yet whose life was to teach the way of salvation to the world. It cannot be other than interesting for the christian to look upon this hallowed place.

The altar of the Innocents, and the room where St. Jerome so long lived, are under the Church of the Nativity. Returning to the convent we find that the monks have prepared a comfortable meal which we partake of with much relish.

Looking toward the east we see the plains of Bethlehem on which the shepherds were watching their flocks by night when the Star of Bethlehem appeared to them; and as if to bring that scene more forcibly to our minds, we see the shepherds in the distance crossing the plain followed by flocks of sheep and goats. On those now dry and verdureless plains Ruth gleaned her scanty harvest of grain.

SACRED GROTTO (BETHLEHEM).

It is three hours ride to Hebron where in the cave of Machpelah lie Sarah and Abraham, Leah and Jacob, Rebekah and Isaac side by side. Some of our company go down to the Pools of Solomon.

After one more examination of the interior of the Church of the Nativity at Bethlehem, in the course of which an Arab school is exhibited which is attached to the convent, we return to our horses. Here is a motley crowd, some begging *bakshish*, others endeavoring to sell us curiosities; for an extensive business is carried on among the Bethlehemites who make various articles from the mother of pearl brought from the Red Sea, and offer them for sale to Pilgrims. We ride swiftly out of the city of David, and urge our horses over the shepherd's plain to Jerusalem.

My Christmas days will ever be more precious as my thoughts revert back to Bethlehem, where Christmas had its birth.

CHAPTER XXXVII.

THE DEAD SEA.

NOT feeling very well for the past two or three days, and the weather being warm, I have concluded that I will not go down to the Jordan and Dead Sea, but remain with our kind hostess. Mr. G—— will tell the story.

Filing out of the east gate of Jerusalem, down into the Valley of Jehoshaphat, by the Garden of Gethsemane, and up the mount of Olives, we are soon at Bethany, where the *sheiks* who had been previously engaged in Jerusalem, and who were to act as our escort and guard to the Jordan country, came riding swiftly around the village to meet us. They were dressed in full Bedouin costume, with brilliant colored Damascus silk *burnous*, or head-

DEAD SEA.

dress, fastened around their heads with a heavy silk cord. In their girdles were any number of pistols and knives, and each one carried a long firelock. They were mounted upon fine horses, and as they took their place at the head of our train they seemed possessed with the feeling that their position was one of infinite importance.

Leaving Bethany, we descended the rocky sides of a mountain for a half an hour, until we came to a fountain called *El Haud*, which is upon the ancient dividing line between the land of Benjamin and Judah.

As the sun had now risen high in the heavens, and shone with unusual fierceness, we remained for some time by *El Haud*, where Nijem spread our lunch upon the ground in the cool shadow of a high rock. One must travel in the east to realize the blessing "of the shadow of a great rock in a weary land." Again in the saddle, we commenced a journey of seven long hours, through the most desolate tract of country it has ever been my lot to behold. Our path lay along the stony bed of some stream, through narrow defiles, over barren hills, and through deep gorges. We saw no sign of life except two eagles which flew from a high cliff. One of the Arab *sheiks* fired at them, but missed his aim. They calmly soared above us for a long time, as if curious to know for what reason we had invaded their domain.

About half way down to Jericho are the remains of an old stone tower, indicating the traditional scene of the parable of the good Samaritan. This is the wilderness where John preached, and where Christ "fasted forty days and forty nights." As our caravan moved over the last mountain before descending to the plains of Gilgal, the path lay close to the edge of a deep gorge, five hundred feet deep. Down in this is the brook Cherith. Near to the bottom of the precipice the sides of the rocks are perforated with holes or caves. It was in one of these that the Prophet Elijah lived when he was fed by the ravens during the terrible famine which then raged in Palestine. In later years we are told that monks who wish to seclude themselves from the world, secrete themselves in these caves and end their lives in loneliness.

Descending upon the plain, we rode over the ruins of ancient Jericho. All that can be seen of that once mighty city is a small portion of the remains of the aqueduct. The wall around which the priests marched seven times, and blew the rams' horns, is level with the ground. The amphitheatre, where the wicked Herod paraded himself dressed in his royal robes before the people, and the house of Rahab, where she concealed the spies from Israel, are no more. Turning to the northward, along the base of Quarantania, we halted by the fountain of Elisha. These waters, which were so bitter and poisonous before the prophet healed them, are now pure and wholesome. Driving the horses into the water, they were glad to take a long and refreshing draught after their wearisome journey.

Following our dragoman and *sheiks* over the plain, we pitched our camp near to a wretched Bedouin village, called Riha. At one and a half o'clock in the morning the camp is aroused and we move toward the Dead Sea. Traveling over crusted layers of sand for two long hours, just as the first rays of the morning sun came shooting up over the mountains of Moab, we reach the greatest natural wonder of the globe. All the stories of my youth about this sea came rushing vividly upon my mind. It is supposed to cover the plains where stood the cities of Sodom and Gomorrah, being over four thousand feet below Jerusalem, and almost one thousand three hundred feet below the level of the sea. It is the lowest point on the earth's surface. The Jordan and other streams empty into it, but no outlet has ever been discovered. The fish that float down out of the Jordan as soon as they enter the Dead Sea die and come to the surface. The water is so dense that nothing can live in it.

Stories are told by travelers, that birds flying over it die and drop into the water. Poets sing of the "Dead Sea apple," which is fair to the eye, but as soon as it is taken into the hand crumbles to ashes.

We are soon into the water, and find that we can recline upon it with the greatest ease. Even the hand or foot plunged down would be gently buoyed to the surface like a cork. It seemed like being upon a sea of glass, and the pebbly bottom could be seen far down through the crystal water. In a storm, the water rolls like oil, without splashing.

As the sun arose, a more dreary waste could not be imagined. On both sides the sea is bounded by high walls of dull, grey, rugged mountains, and a tree or shrub of any kind cannot exist near its waters. As the sun rides over in the heavens, its reflection upon the water has the peculiar effect of changing the hue of the Dead Sea several times. We came out of the water with a slight burning and smarting of the flesh, which lasted some hours. The air began to be oppressive, and we were glad to get away from the scene of desolation.

CHAPTER XXXVIII.

RIVER JORDAN.

BEFORE the sun had reached its zenith we arrive at the Pilgrim's Ford of the River Jordan, so named from the fact of its being the place where all pilgrims go to bathe.

This place is made hallowed by many sacred associations. The Holy word informs us that the children of Israel after their journey of forty years in the wilderness passed over into the land of Canaan "right against Jericho." At this ford the waters have been divided three times; first, for the passage of Israel; second, when Elijah and Elisha crossed to the other side where the former let his mantle fall upon the latter, and ascended to Heaven; and third, for the return of Elisha. Here Christ was baptized, and the haughty Naaman was sent to dip three times.

PILGRIM'S FORD—RIVER JORDAN.

Hither come pilgrims once a year in great numbers to bathe. Our dragoman told me that two years before he saw a caravan of seventeen thousand pilgrims come down to the Jordan and plunge in.

The river is narrow and swift. It rises in the Anti-Lebanon mountains, and flowing down through the lake of Tiberias, empties into the Dead Sea. Leaving our horses in charge of Nijem, we soon go through the ceremony of dipping three times, and by wading and swimming against the swift current, are soon on the other side. Climbing up the opposite bank and looking back, the first thoughts that came to my mind were of the hymn which I had many times sung—

> "Sweet fields beyond the swelling flood
> Stand dressed in living green;
> So to the Jews old Canaan stood
> While Jordan rolled between."

I shall never hear that hymn sung without being carried back to the hour, when I stood "on the other side of Jordan." To the east lay the plain where the children of Israel were so long encamped, while Moses gave them the Law; and also Mount Pisgah, from the summit of which Moses was permitted to view the promised land before he died.

Of course we filled our cans with Jordan water, as every pilgrim is expected to bring some home with him.

While in bathing a large company of Bedouins came down the opposite bank and crossed the stream. The train of camels which they had with them being able to easily ford the river. They had come from the mountains east and were on their way south toward Egypt. Our Dragoman entered into conversation with them and ascertained that they belonged to a friendly tribe. They pointed over the mountains, and said that a battle had taken place over there between two hostile tribes of Bedouins three days before, and as they came by many of the slain were lying upon the battle-field. Their appearance was much like the Camanche Indians of our own country; and we were not displeased when we saw them repack their camels, and disappear across the plains toward the Dead Sea.

The banks of the river Jordan are lined with a thick growth of bushes, and among them grows the celebrated Balsam tree, which was considered by the ancient nations who inhabited this country to possess a medicinal virtue; and we are told that Anthony, for the sake of the tree, made a present of the plains of the Jordan to Cleopatra. Here also grows the luxuriant Oleander to the size of a tree. The heat is almost unbearable and has a very enervating effect. We slowly return to the camp where we stretch ourselves under the fig trees, lying with our handkerchiefs wet and placed upon our heads, while one of the company reads to us the story of the crossing of the children of Israel with the ark of the covenant, and of the setting up of the twelve monumental stones, to commemorate God's goodness in dividing the waters and bringing the Israelites safely into the land of Canaan.

As the eye sweeps around the vast and desolate plain, which was once occupied by tramping millions, the land that "flowed with milk and honey," it requires no stretch of the imagination to realize that the curse of God has been fulfilled. On the south is the dreary waste of the Dead Sea; to the west are the barren hills of Judea, among which can be seen the Mount of Temptation, on the top of which Satan offered the kingdoms of the world to the Son of God if he would bow down and worship him; to the north and east is the great valley of the Jordan and the land of Moab, and also toward the east the land where once stood the "Giant cities of Bashan."

Meditating upon this grand and solitary scene, we prepare ourselves for the last night upon the plain and decide to start at daylight for Jerusalem.

CHAPTER XXXIX.

BEDOUIN ARABS.

SCARCELY had we fallen asleep before we were awakened by a wild humming sound outside of the tents, and going out we find about a dozen Bedouin Arabs dancing a war dance around the cook's fire, brandishing swords which they carried with them, and making night hideous with their howling.

Their purpose was soon made known; they demanded *bakshish* for the performance. Passing around the hat a purse was made up for them and through the influence of the *sheiks* they were induced to retire. Their voices could be heard shouting at a great distance as they went away.

No sooner had we laid down again than we were as quickly disturbed by the rapid galloping of horsemen into the camp. They were friendly Arabs who came to notify us that a large body of Bedouins were in the vicinity. By firing their guns they roused the inhabitants of the little village of Riha near by, and the women and children came excitedly into an enclosure adjoining the watch-tower. On the top of this tower a fire was kindled, which illuminated the darkness for miles around. It was less than half an hour from the arrival of the Arabs before the inhabitants of Riha were in a state of defense. Assured that under these circumstances there was little chance for rest this night, we struck camp and long before morning dawned, were ascending the first mountain on our way to Jerusalem. As we were threading our way over the rocks a stranger joined our caravan; and soon another, and another, until several savage looking Bedouins were walking barefooted among our horses. The only garment which they wore was a coarse heavy blanket thrown around them, but each was well armed with gun and war club.

Not a word was spoken by any one, suddenly

they disappeared in the darkness. Once more they came and departed in the same mysterious manner. After which we could hear them on the hills singing their wild Arabic songs and calling to one another.

Our path was for a half a mile through a deep gorge, and when near the darkest part guns were fired over our heads. As we came out on the other side of the mountain, these savages rushed down upon us with a yell resembling an Indian war whoop, catching the horses bridles they said we had gold, and must give it to them or they would take it from us. Our *sheiks* now sprang forward to the front, when there commenced a series of manœuvres which lasted several minutes, and if they were not dangerous, they were certainly interesting to us, who calmly waited to see the result.

They would talk and gesticulate in the most violent manner, and often place the muzzles of their guns close to each other's heads as if to fire, then put them down, and again with swords and war clubs dash up to one another. The conflict appeared on the verge of commencing several times. After this exciting wrangle had continued for some time the robbers slowly retreated back into the mountains and we were allowed to proceed. The probability is that many of these demonstrations are gotten up for the purpose of extorting money from travelers without the intent of murder or violence. Allowing this to be true, I will venture the assertion, that, if we had not outnumbered them, and been too well armed, they would have appropriated to their own use what little spare change we had with us, even if they had been compelled to resort to a dishonorable method to obtain it.

The Bedouin Arabs live in small villages, or wander in caravans making their abode wherever night overtakes them. Their wealth generally consists in the number of camels, horses, sheep, or goats which they possess. They divide themselves into tribes and these frequently attack one another with great fury, sometimes from one cause and sometimes from another, and when it is for the purpose of robbery the victorious party will drive off with them all the flocks belonging to the defeated tribe. They are splendid horsemen. They generally ride upon a gallop, and they can fire their guns with great precision, although going at full speed.

Their women are made to do the drudgery, and are the slaves of the men. They paint and tatoo their faces, making themselves as hideous as the South Sea Islanders.

The Bedouin Arab often thinks more of his horse than of his wife. Give him a piece of bread and he will share it with his horse. These animals are small, graceful, and kind, and when going fast always gallop, as they are never trained to trot.

The Turkish government have not much control over these people, excepting those along the sea-coast.

I was informed that the only way the Sultan could collect the taxes from the various tribes inhabiting the country east of the Dead Sea and mountains of Moab, was to send among them an army to take possession of whatever they could find; principally camels and horses, which they would drive to the cities along the sea-coast.

Reaching the fountain of El Haud, we toiled up the mountain to Bethany, where we discharged our escort, and spurring our jaded horses around the southern crest of the Mount of Olives, the Holy City came again in sight. On the mountains round about could be seen the camps, not of the Roman army, but of the Quaker City Pilgrims, who now began to arrive in small companies from the different parts of Palestine.

CHAPTER XL.

RETURN TO THE SHIP.

TO-DAY, Miss B—— and myself are seated in the door of our tent, bargaining with the sellers of curiously wrought articles of olive-wood and pearl. They are Arabs who have come out of the city to dispose of their wares, and are extremely persistent in their efforts to trade. One aged Arab is offering for sale some tiny goblets, which he declares are made from an olive tree cut from the Mount of Olives; and to prevent our disbelief in his story, produces a written statement, bearing the stamp and seal of some consul, to the purport that we might believe any thing which the bearer asserted. Suffice to say, we made selections of his goods, and he left, bestowing a plenitude of good will and wishes upon us.

One after another of the Pilgrim camps vanish, as the time has come for them to be marching to the sea, Nijem has given the order that we must be in readiness at daylight. We make one more trip through the city, and around outside of the walls. The following morning, as the first rays of morning light dawned over Mount Olivet, we turn upon our horses, and take a farewell look of the City of the Great King — the city where were enacted such thrilling events at the commencement of the Christian era — the central figure being Christ, about which the great Jewish historian makes mention in these words:

"Now, there was about this time Jesus, a wise man, if it be lawful to call him a man, for he was a doer of wonderful works — a teacher of such men as receive the truth with pleasure. He drew over to him both many of the Jews and many of the Gentiles. He was [the] Christ; and when Pilate, at the suggestion of the principal men amongst us, had condemned him to the cross, those that loved him at the first did not forsake him, for he appeared to them alive again the third day, as the divine prophets had foretold, these and ten thousand other wonderful things concerning him; and the tribe of Christians, so named from him, are not extinct to this day."

As we bid adieu to Palestine, I will record the lesson which I have learned.

It is a rocky and desolate land. The inhabitants are poor and deprived of the advantages of the society and refinement which exist under the more civilized governments of the world: but a visit to this country cannot fail to stamp upon the mind of the pilgrim the truth of the Bible. Whenever a description of a place, or location of a valley, mountain, hill, or city is mentioned in the Holy Word, by comparison and examination the truth of the statement will be verified. Many things have thus been explained to my mind, which I have never understood before.

"Two women shall be grinding at a mill; the one shall be taken, and the other left." "Two shall be upon the house top." "The shepherd goeth before his sheep, and the sheep follow him, for they know his voice." All these passages of scripture, and many more, are illustrated by the manners and customs of the people, which are the same now as they were thousands of years ago; and if I had never been a believer in the sacred Word, I am sure that I should leave Jerusalem with a firm conviction of the truth of the story of Christ, and the Christian religion.

We are once more on board our floating home, and it is pleasant to see the sun-browned faces of the Pilgrims, as they return from their long and arduous journeyings. Some of the ladies are pretty well tired out, and express themselves satisfied that they have reached the ship where they can rest. I am confident that our ship never looked so inviting to me as it now does upon my return from the pilgrimage. There have been no mishaps and no deaths, therefore no faces are missing.

Our ship's company is enlarged by the addition of most of the Jaffa colonists, who have made arrangements to go on our steamer to Egypt, and from there ship to Southampton. Ere this, I presume they have reached America, wiser and better people.

Our course was now toward Alexandria, Egypt, which we reached in two days.

How quickly all are on deck to get the first view of the city founded by Alexander the Great — the most important sea-port of the Mediterranean. Taking a pilot on board, our steamer is guided up the narrow and dangerous channel.

As we near the level and sandy shores, the Viceroy's palace and the Pillar of Diocletian appear in the distance.

The light of day fades away and the stars come out one by one, as we glide among the ships of all nations and let go the anchor near to an Egyptian man-of-war. Around us are hundreds of lights sparkling and dancing upon the waters.

CHAPTER XLI.

EGYPT.

EGYPTIAN donkeys and boys, both about the same height, are our first introduction to Alexandria. There is such a swarm of them we can hardly land The boys are shouting vociferously, "Good donkey! fine donkey! have a ride." These little animals are the most important conveyance in the city. At every turn they come trotting or jumping along with their heavy burdens, while the boys are running behind, and urging them forward with blows and shouts.

There is no time to be wasted, and we proceed at once to explore the city. There is something invigorating in the life and stir around us after our long and tiresome journey.

In the center of the city is the "*Esbekiyeh,*" or square, filled with trees. Around this runs a broad street lined with banking-houses, and shops whose windows are filled with European goods.

The ancient Pillar of Diocletian, or Pompey's Pillar, stands now outside of the walls of the city; but the spot was once the center of Alexandria. It is over ninety feet high, and was erected in the third century, in honor of Diocletian. This column is formed of one immense block of red Egyptian granite, a stone on which time makes but little impression.

The Catacombs well reward the investigation of the curious antiquary. Many of these tombs have been opened and divested of their contents. In them have been discovered relics which date back thousands of years. The Catacombs of Egypt are more vast in extent than any in the world. The most ancient are those of the Kings of Thebes. It is believed that the Egyptians spent such sums of money upon embalming and upon magnificent sepulchres, because they had faith in the literal resurrection of the body, if it were preserved from decay. The richest and costliest of the catacombs are completely covered in their interior by sculptured hieroglyphics, and by paintings in fresco which, when found free from the desecrations of the Arabs, "are as fresh as if laid on but yesterday," and the colors are extremely brilliant, although thousands of years old. The sculptures and the frescoes represent all the scenes of Egyptian history, as well as their ceremonies and customs, from the coronation of a monarch to a child among his toys.

The entrances to the catacombs of Thebes are simply by a gate, in a square frame which surrounds the subterranean opening. You descend first into one vast area filled with chambers containing the stone coffins of the mummies, then far into another, and then again into still lower deeps among the dead of ages ago. "The entire chain of mountains in the neighborhood of Thebes," says one writer, "is mined by an immense number of catacombs. It is calculated that during the ages when the art of mummification was known and practiced, not less than 400,000,000 of mummies were entombed in the Egyptian catacombs!"

This, not of Egypt entire, but of one single city of Egypt. The catacombs of Rome have never yet been fully explored; but it is said that many of them were made long before the Rome of Romulus and Remus, and that all the Seven Hills are honeycombed with passages, dark corridors, and galleries, where the sunshine never enters.

Here we see evidences of the early history of the world, for no land has such a historical record as Egypt. It is the country where lived the builders of the Pyramids, where dwelt the Pharaohs, and where Jacob visited his long lost son Joseph; the land from which the children of Israel marched forth from their oppressors, and the country to which Joseph and Mary fled with the infant Christ.

Cleopatra's Needles, another monument of the ancient splendor of Egypt, is standing in Alexandria. There were two, standing side by side. One of them was presented by the Pacha some years ago to England, and the attempt was made to convey it to Trafalgar Square, London. They succeeded in lowering it to the ground, where it lies buried in the sand to this day. It is truly wonderful how these great pillars and blocks of stone in Ephesus, Baalbec, Jerusalem, and Egypt, were moved to the positions where they now are. Many of them are monoliths—solid squares of stone or marble, fifty to sixty feet in length, and ten to fifteen feet in diameter, weighing thousands of tons. These great blocks in some cases were chiseled from the quarries and carried hundreds of miles, then were lifted into walls or posited upon pedestals at a considerable elevation from the ground. Have not some of the arts of the world known to former generations passed away? At the present time, with all the science, skill, and machinery known to man, these enormous weights could scarcely be moved.

The Obelisk standing is of the same material as Pompey's Pillar, and covered with hieroglyphics. It is over seventy feet in height. These needles are supposed to have been brought by one of the Cæsars from the city of Heliopolis. The position which they now occupy was in front of Cæsar's palace, and they were called Cleopatra's needles in honor of the Egyptian Queen.

We have ridden around the city, and along the banks of the Nile, passing many beautiful gardens filled with date and banana trees with luxuriant bunches of the delicious fruit ripening upon them.

The Egyptian dates are the finest we have found. They grow exceedingly large, and form an important article of export. On the banks of the Nile are large numbers of the *fellaheen*, employed in various ways. At one time we make our way amid camels with their wide-spreading loads, and anon trains of donkeys on which are panniers filled with grass or bearing goat-skins full of water. Wells are far less common in the East than with us, and water-carriers are in constant demand. They frequently bear picturesque vases of water strapped to their backs. These have a spout near the handles of the vase, and when the carrier wishes to fill a cup or other vessel, he stoops forward and the cup is soon filled. The forms of some of these vases have not materially changed for ages.

Women and boys are trudging along carrying dates. Many of the women convey their children upon their shoulders, the child holding fast to its mother's head to steady itself, while older ones will balance themselves in this position, looking around quite unconcerned. A different mode of treating the infant prevails in Italy. There it is secured to a pillow, looking much like a mummy, or bound to a board and carried on the mother's back, or hung upon a tree while she works in the fields.

The Egyptian women are in the habit of carrying burdens on their heads, which gives them a straight and lofty carriage. Their greatest care is to conceal their faces.

One is not surprised that plagues sweep over this land with such terrible fury, when he observes the extreme want of cleanliness which exists among the people. The children often have but one ragged article of clothing about them, the upper part of the body being entirely exposed to the sun and Sirocco winds. It is not uncommon to see females similarly clothed.

Many of the streets of Alexandria are extremely narrow, and the houses are built over the streets, each story projecting over the one below, so that the tops nearly meet. This makes the streets cool, as they are thus protected from the sun's rays. The windows are latticed in lieu of glass. In some places old pieces of matting or canvass are put up under which the people collect. Here they are sheltered from the sun while they smoke, talk, and sleep.

The money-changers are walking along with a bag of francs in one hand and Egyptian silver pieces in the other, which they chink and toss in the air; meanwhile calling to the people to know if they wish their money changed.

CHAPTER XLII.

LEAVING THE PILGRIMS.

ISMAEL Pacha, the Khe-dive of Egypt, rules nearly four millions of people. His government is an absolute monarchy like that of the Sultan, to whom he reports once a year. He is much more liberal in his views than the Sultan and is more ready to introduce and adopt the manners and customs of more civilized nations Thus in Egypt we see railroads and manufactories running by steam. Machinery of the most approved kinds is now being brought to Egypt, and before many years Alexandria bids fair to rank in enterprise and commerce among the first cities of the world.

In appearance the Viceroy is dark and somewhat lighter built than the Sultan. His face wears a look

VICEROY'S PALACE.

of considerable intelligence and activity. He wears the inevitable *fez* and a European suit of black.

Mr. G—— has been fortunate enough to obtain permission to visit the Viceroy's palace. It is a large, highly decorated and showy structure. Adjoining is the Harem. Many of the rooms in the palace are so richly adorned in Oriental style, that they strikingly remind one of the deeds of good genii in the *Arabian Nights*. At almost every door, we pass a Nubian guard. We are informed that the Viceroy selects these Nubians for the most trusty positions for the reason that they make more faithful servants than the native Egyptians.

In a large square belonging to the palace are several companies of soldiers, dressed in bright zouave uniforms and going through with their daily drill. In one of the rooms of the court building we witnessed the trial of several prisoners for petty crimes. Each culprit was brought in by an armed guard and placed before the high officer or judge, who was sitting cross-legged upon a broad crimson divan. The coffee and pipe was often handed to him during his arduous labor. Without scarcely lifting his eyes to the prisoner he would silently listen to the recounting of his crime by witnesses. After which in a few words he would pronounce the sentence, when the unfortunate criminal would be hurried away by the soldiers, and another brought to take his place.

The Viceroy frequently goes out to ride in a splendid European carriage which he keeps for his ostentatious use. A loud cracking of a whip and the shouting of a groom announce to the dispersing crowd the approach of the Magnate. Several gaudily dressed horsemen go prancing by, followed by the Pacha seated in his luxurious carriage drawn by six fine Arabian horses. After which follow other horsemen which complete the retinue.

With eager steps the Pilgrims now press forward to the Pyramids, Cairo "the city of Victory," and other places. Two have decided to return to America by the way of Marseilles, and have already left on a French steamer. One has sailed for Southampton, and two more have already gone to Constantinople. We have determined to change the route of our journey, and instead of accompanying the *Quaker City* to Valencia, Spain, as our passage ticket entitles us to do, we have concluded to bid good-bye to our friends and sail for Corfu as we wish to see more of the continent of Europe before we return.

One of the Austrian Lloyd steamers is anchored near us, and is about to sail for Corfu. We row out to her to get an idea of her accommodations and are greatly pleased with her appearance. She is an elegant new iron steamship, and superbly fitted up, besides being extremely neat and comfortable. We return to the shore and at the office of the steamship company engage our passage on the *Apollo*.

In parting from the *Quaker City*, which has been our floating home for months, I have only the pleasantest of recollections. My lady friends of the party I shall certainly remember with the kindest regard. They have been obliging and courteous, and the time spent in their society has been very pleasant indeed.

There might readily be given reasons for and against so large a company traveling over the world together; but while we have been with the Pilgrims in the East the time has passed away pleasantly and profitably. To be sure the *Quaker City* was not loaded with a gay and giddy throng. They were mostly persons of middle age gathered from various parts of America, and as a general thing intelligent, aspiring for information, and accustomed to wealth and refinement.

It is full as well for one to be considerate while wandering over the ruins of the ancient cities of the world, and walking amid the sacred places of Christianity; however, I think none of the voyagers will ever look back upon their journey with regret, even though the *great excursion* bears the stamp of sobriety and moderation.

After the final leave taking we are soon on board the *Apollo* bound for Corfu.

CHAPTER XLIII.

THE VOYAGE.

SLEEPING soundly and sweetly all night, I arose early and looked out of the stateroom window. The sun was just rising out of the beautiful blue waters of the Mediterranean. Afar off on the waves the early sunlight is dancing and flashing, spreading a golden lustre upon the bosom of the deep.

We have coffee at seven and breakfast at ten o'clock.

The passengers all appear strange to us. They are composed of Egyptians, Turks, Greeks, and a few from India on their way to Germany and England. I formed an acquaintance with a very estimable and cultured India lady, who is going on a visit to Germany in company with her husband and child. She took much interest in explaining to me the manners and customs of the people of India, also giving us valuable information about the missionary work there. I was much interested in her description of their passage through the Red Sea. The weather was intensely warm, seriously affecting the passengers and resulting in the death of one, a not unusual circumstance on the passage.

A young couple who had been recently married in Bombay, had taken passage on the same steamer. They were going to Austria to see the relatives of the groom, whom he had not seen for many years.

The groom was suddenly taken ill and died. After a few simple ceremonies, amid the gloom of the ship and the heart-rending grief of the bride, the body was lowered into the deep.

There was much sympathy manifested among the passengers for the beautiful but unfortunate India bride.

> "Weep for the life-charm early flown,
> The spirit broken, bleeding and alone."

A generous collection was taken up and pre-

THE VOYAGE. 331

sented her, and every possible assistance was rendered her by the voyagers.

To-day is a charming one on land and sea; and as we glide along close to the island of Candia every little while one of the Turkish blockading fleet comes in sight.

The lofty mountains of the island are on our right in which are secreted the noble Cretans who have battled so long and suffered so much for their liberty. We sweep swiftly by the island of Cerigo, and by Navarino where the great naval battle was fought between the Turks and English; pass the islands of Zante and Cephalonia, and the next day at ten o'clock, rounding the high rocky point on which stands an old Roman fort, we sighted the city of Corfu.

The fort is hewn out of solid rock, and looks picturesque, being completely overgrown with vines and shrubs.

The island of Corfu is one of the largest in the Ionian sea. It is thickly populated and has an abundance of fruit. The oranges are exceedingly fine. Here we have a refreshing shower of rain; the first which we have seen for over five months.

From Corfu we sail through the Adriatic Sea for Trieste, Austria. For a long distance the shore presents a peculiar appearance. Mountains of rock rise perpendicular to a great height out of the sea.

The weather is changing rapidly as we steam to the northward, and the light clothing adapted to the Egyptian climate must be laid aside, and thick warm garments substituted, as we near the colder latitude of Austria.

We are soon out of sight of land. For two days and nights our splendid steamer has been struggling in the Adriatic. The storm has been fearful. It is the time of the year our captain informs us when the *Borea* sweeps down from the Alpine mountains upon the Adriatic sea with terrible fury. Great foaming waves would wash over the steamer, carrying away anything not strongly secured to the deck. The passengers are compelled to remain in their berths below and hold on firmly to keep themselves from being dashed to and fro. The pilots are lashed to the wheel, and the loud roar of the hurricane through the rigging drowns ever other sound.

The Adriatic is noted for these gales. On the morning of the sixth day after leaving Egypt our staunch steamer plowed her way into the harbor of Trieste.

Coming safely through such a terrific gale leads me to notice how well adapted and constructed these powerful iron steamships are for trying service on the sea. Whole fleets of them are already in possession of Austria, Egypt, and even Turkey. My own great country with all its immense resources is far inferior in its ocean service.

Taking rooms at the Locanda Grande we are glad once more to be on terra firma, after five days sailing. Again we are among a people who dress in European style. It seems strange not to see and hear the clamor of the turbaned Turks and Arabs to whom we have become so accustomed.

In the large square fronting our hotel is the statue of Charles the Sixth, and a curious fountain. Near by is the market square in which are two or three hundred men and women with stands in front of them, on which are placed scales, as all the fruits and vegetables are sold by weight.

The women wear short petticoats, and kerchiefs about their heads, and are quite tidy and neat.

Trieste is the most important Austrian city on the Adriatic. It is a fine commercial port, and has an extensive canal, large enough to admit ordinary vessels, which penetrates to the heart of the city. We give the Exchange, Opera-house, and Catholic Cathedral a call. The latter has some very fine paintings.

To-day a feeling of sadness comes over me, like a cloud in the calm clear sky. I am thinking of home. It is the sixth anniversary of my dear sister's death—the first that I have missed placing my tribute of flowers upon her grave.

The castle of Miramar, the residence of the late Emperor Maximilian, stands just out of Trieste, admirably situated upon the shore of the Adriatic. It is a very handsome place with extensive grounds. The castle is partly closed and left in care of the servants, as the Empress Carlotta is staying with her sister in Belgium.

The people here speak in praise of the unfortunate Maximilian. Evidently he was a much greater favorite with the Austrians than his brother the present Emperor Francis Joseph.

CHAPTER XLIV.

CAVE OF ADELSBERG.

THE early morning train brings us from Trieste, along the shore of the Adriatic, and through the mountains and valleys of Styria, to the little town of Adelsberg where is to be seen one of the greatest natural excavations of the Old World.

At the office of the Grotto we are required to register our names and pay the fee, which is from ten to fifteen dollars, according to the number of guides which attend you. We employ five, the usual number. Each one carries a basket filled with candles, as we are to have a "grand illumination" which requires about three hundred lights.

This wonderful Grotto was discovered in the eleventh century, and soon became celebrated for the splendor and richness of its interior. It is composed of many caverns which have been found at different times. The most notable are named "The Cathedral," "Ball Room," "Behind the Mummies," Belvidere," and "Calvary Mountain."

In the Ball Room, which is a half a mile under the mountain, a ball is given on Whitsuntide Monday by the surrounding peasantry. At this time the Emperor visits the caverns which are illuminated by many thousand lights.

Wrapped in thick warm clothing and accompanied by the guides we enter the first cavern beside the river Peik. Following its course for some distance under the mountain, it plunges its foaming flood over the inflexible rocks with a wild and almost deafening roar. The darkness and gloom, the reflection of our lights in the rushing water, form a scene long to be remembered. Suddenly the river disappears in the earth and is seen no more.

Following our guides through Ferdinand's Grotto we come into one called St. Peter's Chair, where the stalactites are combined in such a manner as to resemble St. Peter's chair at Rome. The Ball-

Room has a spacious floor on which many hundred couples of the young peasantry can dance at once, while the strains of the band of music echo through the lofty arches of the cavern. The seats for the orchestra have been perfectly formed by nature in the wall high above the floor.

Some of the guides have already illuminated with a hundred lights the Belvidere, and the eye rests upon a grand formation of stalactites. Transparent curtains are waving down in light folds. In a niche is a group of children apparently asleep. In another part of the cave a beautiful spring falls like a silver ribbon thirty feet upon the crystal pavement below. A monument has been erected here in honor of Francis Joseph First and his consort the Empress Elizabeth. In the cave justly called the "Flower Garden" are represented by stalactites and stalagmites, thousands of flowers of purest white— above, below, on either side we step among them, seemingly transported to some enchanted fairy land. One cannot form a just conception of the impressive beauty of this spot without seeing it.

After wandering through grotto after grotto each one more beautiful than the others, we return from the subterranean world to the light of day, fully satisfied that it would be in vain to endeavor to depict the innumerable variations in the groups and formations which nature has displayed in the beautiful stalactites and stalagmites of the different caverns of this wonderful grotto.

Returning to the hotel we find the village peasantry assembling in the large saloon around small tables, to while away the evening hours. Many well dressed ladies and gentlemen are playing various games and merrily talking. The tables are loaded with glasses which are often filled with foaming beer. The ladies seem to enjoy drinking it as much as the gentlemen. The whole forms an interesting picture of German life.

The railroad from here to Vienna runs over the Styrian Alps or Semmering mountains. This road was built at an expense of over one hundred million of dollars. Its length is three hundred and sixty miles, and it is a most extraordinary piece of engineering. The difficulty in carrying this road over the Alps is shown by its being necessary to cut fourteen different tunnels through the rock, in a distance of less than two miles. At one moment we are crossing a deep valley, at another, running along the edge of a dizzy precipice, over which the merest accident would throw the train and dash it to atoms. At another time we are flying along among the snow and ice on the tops of the Semmering mountains, and then for a long time descend with lightning speed, depending entirely upon the breaks for our safety; and yet we are told that an accident seldom happens, so much care and precaution are bestowed upon the management of this road.

At the pleasant town of Gratz on the river Mur, we find the people sociable and thrifty. It is quite a rich and aristocratic place, and we had been informed that it was celebrated for the beauty of its females. Of course I was on the *qui vive* to see them, but I could not detect their superiority in this respect.

GRAPE GATHERING IN AUSTRIA.

The country from here to Vienna is finely cultivated. It being Autumn the peasantry are industriously gathering the plentiful crops. Men and women are at work in the fields together.

Along the wayside, as in Italy and France, are numerous shrines for the laborer and traveler, in front of which we frequently see some poor peasant kneeling at his devotions.

While meditating upon the varied scenes which pass by like a panorama as we speed along, the imposing city of Vienna looms up in the distance.

CHAPTER XLV.

VIENNA.

VIENNA is to Austria what Paris is to France. The Austrians term it the Emperor's city. The streets are spacious and well laid out, and are lined with fine stores filled with rich goods.

The Viennese are out on the streets or promenading on the *Bastei*, giving the city a gay and lively appearance.

We are delightfully situated at the *Kaiserin Elizabeth* and feel quite at home.

Vienna is located on a plain on the south side of the dark rolling waters of the Danube. It is surrounded by strong fortifications and has been the theatre of many a sanguinary conflict. It has been contended for by the Romans, the Goths, and subse-

SCENE ON THE DANUBE.

quently Charlemagne obtained possession of it. The saying is that over two millions have been slain upon the battle-field of Vienna.

Some days are busily occupied with its churches, palaces, galleries, shops, and parks. Among the latter the Prater is the most frequented by equestrians and carriages, many of which are very elegant, reminding one of Hyde Park, London. This park is four miles in length, and bounded by two branches of the Danube. It is threaded with carriage roads and foot walks, contains a number of cafés and pavilions, and when thronged with people looks like an enchanted forest.

The Austrians consider the Danube the finest river in the world, and certainly there is some excuse for their pride in this noble stream, second in size to the Volga alone in all Europe. It rises somewhere in the Black Forest, and after a tortuous course of 1,770 miles empties into the Black Sea. From Passau to Lintz the scenery about the Danube excels in sombre grandeur anything to be seen on the Rhine. It is a dangerous river to navigate on account of the reefs, whirlpools, and the rapidity of its current. Its course from Lintz to Vienna is not swift however, and very peaceful and rustic farming scenes delight the eye of the traveler.

At breakfast we are agreeably surprised by meeting a general and his charming wife from America, who had traveled with us in England, and were now on their way to Italy, intending to remain in Europe for two or three years.

What a glorious morning, the sky is clear, the weather lovely, and all nature full of joy. We improve it by driving to the Palace of Schonbrunn just outside of the city, the summer residence of Francis Joseph and Elizabeth—the Emperor and Empress. There Maria Theresa resided, and Napoleon when in Austria. The Duke of Reichstadt lived and died there. The palace is decorated with paintings, gilding, and statuary. In the garden of the palace Stapps the German student attempted to assassinate the French Emperor.

We could not fail to call the gardens of Schonbrunn delightful. They are shut in by trees trimmed into high walls of varied green and are adorned with *parterres* of brilliant flowers. Scattered here and there are fountains and statues. There are conservatories for rare and exotic plants, and also a menagerie. At the end of the garden on a hill is the Glorietta Temple, from which is the finest view in the environs of Vienna.

We wandered through the long avenues of the park over which large trees are bent and trimmed to meet, forming a shady bower for miles in length.

At the foot of the Glorietta hill is the beautiful fountain of Schonobrunnen. Near the palace is a small hotel where we dine in true German style. Instead of coffee or tea every one drinks beer and wine. The Austrians enjoy their meals heartily, sitting for a long time at the table, each one endeavoring to be sociable and entertaining.

Last evening we attended the opera at the Grand Opera House. It was crowded with the *beau monde* of Vienna, many of the gentlemen were in military uniforms.

The opera, which was *Zampa*, was rendered

finely, being accompanied by an orchestra of over two hundred musicians. The fair Prima Donna being frequently *encored* by the audience, bowed gracefully to their marks of appreciation, but received no bouquets, as that custom is not in vogue with the Viennese. The Opera House is open every night, and always crowded by the music loving and fashionable Viennese people.

No city in Europe boasts of so many resident nobility as Vienna. It has no less than twenty-four princes, sixty or seventy counts, and any number of barons and other titled gentry. A great number of these are always to be seen at the opera, and on the Prater, greatly enjoying life and society.

St. Stephen's Cathedral is a stately and ancient structure, erected almost five centuries ago. Its tower is over four hundred and thirty feet in height and is the most conspicuous object in the city. Among the tombs in the Cathedral are those of Prince Eugene and Frederic the Second. Two hundred and ten figures and over thirty-five coats of arms decorate the tomb of the latter, also the motto of Frederic the Second—*Austria Est Imperare Orbi Universo*. The pulpit is exceedingly unique, the material being of stone and curiously wrought. This being the time of service the grand old organ peals through the high arches thrilling the soul with a grand solemnity.

The church of the Capuchins contains in its vaults the remains of many of the royal blood of Austria. Ringing a bell it is answered by a monk wearing a black gown, who guides us through the vaults. In the center of the first vault are the sarcophagi of Maria Theresa, and Francis the Second. The monk repeats the story that every day, for the last thirteen years of her life, Maria Theresa descended to this vault to mourn by the tomb of her dear Francis.

The casket containing the remains of the Duke of Reichstadt is made of copper and is very plain; the only ornament being a raised cross; beside it is that of his mother, Maria Lousia, and his grandfather, the emperor Francis First, whose dying request was that he might be buried beside his grandson. In a solid silver coffin lie the remains of Joseph the First. In an obscure corner of the vaults by the light of the taper the monk pointed to the tomb of Maria Theresa's Preceptress, as it was the Empress's desire to have her placed in the same vault. Here repose ancestral grandeur and power. There are over one hundred buried in the vaults of the Capuchins. After leaving the Church of the Capuchins we enjoy a stroll amid the busy maze of life and pleasure. The Viennese seem to like nothing so well as to see and be seen. Throngs are sauntering along in front of the jewelry, meerschaum, Bohemian ware and fancy goods stores, and on the *Glacis*. The Belvidere, Egyptian Museum and Imperial Arsenal are crowded with objects of great value and interest. After making purchases at the shops we return to our hotel.

CHAPTER XLVI.

SALZBURG AND MUNICH.

TAKING a *fiacre* we drive through the streets of the Imperial city to the railway station to take the cars for Salzburg *en route* to Munich.

We are ushered into one of the handsomest of waiting rooms we have ever seen. The station is of immense size, built of glass and iron, and its various rooms are adorned with marble statues. The railroad is made beautiful on either side with flower gardens, which extend along the whole route. At distances of one mile are employés of the company, standing by the stone cottages in which they live, holding a bright colored flag as a signal to the engineer that the road is free from danger. These watchmen also cultivate the flowers.

Large sums of money are lavished upon the roads in Germany to beautify the scenery and insure the safety of the traveler. The buildings and bridges connected with the railroads are all constructed of solid masonry, in the most firm and substantial manner. The bed of the road, between the tracks, is strewn with fine white pebbles to prevent the dust from rising as the trains dash along. The cars are more luxuriously upholstered than any which we have yet been in. Many of them are like a richly decorated drawing room.

Arriving at Salzburg, the home of Mozart, we remain a limited time in order to visit the house and monument of the great composer. The house is built of light colored rough stone, is three stories high and wears a time-worn look. On the façade of the house is the name of Mozart, and a gilded lyre. Here in his infancy Mozart showed manifestations of that marvelous taste for music which could not be satisfied until, like Handel and Haydn, he had inscribed his great name upon the roll of immortal fame. It is a singular fact, that the early days and lives of the world's greatest musical composers were spent so near together.

Haydn was a choir boy in St. Stephen's Cathedral in Vienna, and it was in the same city that Mozart, Haydn, and Beethoven lived and wrote their greatest works.

The monument of Mozart stands in front of the house, and is crowned with his statue holding in the right hand a scroll of music.

The noble and erect form, the high forehead, and the placid expression of his face, inspire the beholder with reverence and admiration.

It was here Richard First of England, better known as Cœur de Leon, stopped on his return from the wars of the Crusades in Palestine, and was arrested and imprisoned by the Duke of Austria.

Salzburg is situated on the edge of the Tyrol. The people have many of the characteristics of the Tyrolese, who are noted for their peculiar warm-heartedness and frankness of character. The dress of the women consists of a large hat trimmed with long ribbons, skirts of green, black, or blue with a corsage of variegated colors.

They are passionately fond of music, and as they go by we often hear them singing some rustic air. As we pass they cordially greet us.

The Tyrol is the Switzerland of Austria. In the valleys are the Tyrolese villages, where music and dancing is the frequent pastime of the peasantry.

The Riding School, the Brunnen or fountain, and the Cathedral are all ornaments to Salzburg, which is charmingly located upon the river Salza.

The Cathedral has an air of newness and neatness seldom found. In the porch is a priest with a tiny brush, sprinkling holy water over the devotees as they pass in and out. The interior is decorated by six extraordinary paintings representing Christ bearing the Cross.

From Salzburg we are rapidly borne to Munich, the capital of Bavaria. The Rheinischer Hof, like all the German hotels we have found is scrupulously neat. Most of the waiters are boys from the ages of fifteen to eighteen, who are neatly clothed and polite.

Munich is called one of the most lovely and art-inviting cities of Europe. It abounds in cathedrals and galleries of art. There are in the library over five hundred thousand volumes, among which is Luther's Bible.

The statue of Bavaria is outside of the city. It was modeled by Schwanthaler and is the largest in the world. Together with the lion and the pedestal, it is over one hundred feet in height. A spiral stair case leads into the head of the figure, where eight persons can stand at once. Around the statue is a very elegant colonnade and building called the "Hall of the Heroes."

The two Pinacothek galleries contain the richest collection of paintings in Germany. The most noted being that of the "Deluge" by Schorn. It remains unfinished as the artist died before he completed his work. The Glyptothek is filled with rare sculpture, dating back to the Roman and Grecian schools of art.

This morning, accompanied by our commissioner who is over seventy years of age but intelligent and active, we went to the Royal palace of King Ludwig. Among its attractions is the Kaiserzimmer or suite of rooms once occupied by Charles the Seventh, also the rich chapel and cabinet of mirrors. In one saloon hang the portraits of thirty of the most beautiful women of Munich.

From the saloon of Rudolph of Hapsburg we pass into the Throne Room. The gallery is supported by marble columns, between which are gilded statues representing the various princes of Bavaria. At the end of this grand and gorgeous room is an elevated platform with three steps, which are beautifully carpeted, each carpet being wrought in different patterns.

On the throne is the coronation chair of red velvet, set in frame work of gilt. The King is not quite twenty-five years of age, and is soon to be married. There is only one chair upon the throne but a place is arranged for another as soon as the marriage is consummated.

The finest street in the city is Maximilian Street, being named after the Emperor Maximilian. It is very wide, having both carriage drives and walks on either side. Along the center are flowers, trees, and fountains.

The Munich beer is pronounced the best in Germany. On every street are saloons and gardens where men, women, and children enjoy the favorite German beverage.

To-day we have attended a German fair or festival on the grounds in front of the statue of Bavaria. The trees are decked with flags and garlands, booths and tents are erected, and while a fine band discourses sweet music, the young men and maidens are wandering from table to table, purchasing the tempting fruits or chatting together. Others of the male portion are entering with spirit into the athletic feats, target practice and gymnastic exercises generally.

The Germans appear to be the most contented and happy people we have seen in Europe ; and there is an air of thrift and industry about them which is very pleasant to see. They greatly delight in picnics, fairs, and festivals, which are all conducted in the most quiet and orderly manner.

They do not strive with such care and anxiety to make money, but what little they do earn is used to the best advantage; and whether rich or poor they all seem cheerful.

Before leaving Munich we drive out to the cemetery. A singular custom of the people is to carry all who die to a large building near the entrance to the cemetery. This hall is divided into various apartments by glass partitions; one is set apart for the rich and another for the poor. The bodies are prepared for burial and and placed in coffins more or less elegant, according to the circumstances of the departed. Here they remain generally three days, during which time they are exposed to the view of their relatives and friends. Infancy, youth, and old age sleep side by side Many of the coffins are almost covered with flowers, while throngs come at all hours of the day to gaze sadly through the glass partitions. From two o'clock to five, every day, there is a continual procession of funerals from this building to the cemetery.

CHAPTER XLVII.

BADEN BADEN.

THE scenery from Munich to Baden Baden is diversified and picturesque. The variety of the grand Autumn panorama, not the art of all the painters in the world could imitate. The mountains, forests, and valleys far and wide are brilliant with a thousand colors.

We roll swiftly by the pleasant cities of Augsburg, in Bavaria, Ulm and Stuttgardt, in the kingdom of Wurtemburg, and Carlsruhe, the capital of the Duchy of Baden, until we reach the famous old town of Heidelberg, celebrated for its Castle and University. The latter is attended by over five hundred students, who pride themselves on the eccentric shaped hat which they wear, and in their proficiency in duelling, which until lately was carried to the most reprehensible extent. It was not unfrequent for a student of the university to have three, four, and sometimes even as many as six *affairs d'honneur* on his hands at once. They do not often kill each other, as they fight with a weapon not well adapted to that purpose; but they scar each other's faces in a hideous manner; and what is very singular in this age of refinement at least, is that they are even proud of these evidences of ungentlemanly brawls.

On our left is the Black Forest, which may justly be called one of the most interesting districts of Southern Germany. It is wild and romantic. The tall pines of its forest are sombre and imposing. Here were laid the scenes of the celebrated German legend of Siegfried and numberless other romantic tales.

Arriving at Baden Baden we engage board at the Hotel de Russie where everything is *comme il faut.*

Although the gay season is over, there are many lingering here, and the hotels are tolerably well filled.

This morning is dull and gray, threatening rain;

but it does not deter us from going to the springs, and wandering over this charming spot.

Baden Baden is built upon the slope of a hill on the border of the Black Forest, and by the little river Oos. It is the most fashionable lounge in Europe. Its patrons come from Russia, Austria, France, Italy, England, and America. At all times more or less Americans are to be found here.

There are from ten to fifteen hot springs in the valley, the water of which resembles and tastes much like warm milk, or weak broth. The water is considered very efficacious in healing many diseases, consequently it is a resort for invalids as well as pleasure seekers.

The Trink Halle and Conversationshaus are the centres of attraction. The water is brought from the springs in pipes to the former, where it may be had free at all hours of the day. The fashion concentrates in the afternoon and evening in and around the Conversationshaus. In front has been erected a Pagoda for musical bands, at an expense of fifteen thousand dollars.

The Conversationshaus is brilliantly lighted in the evening, where may be seen the excitement and merriment at its full height. Hundreds are dancing and promenading to the music, while in small saloons contiguous to the ball room are gambling tables, at which are gathered old and young, male and female. As the wheel revolves thousands of dollars are changing hands. This opens a new leaf in the history of my life, as it is the first time I have ever seen a gaming table. Hundreds are watching the game with anxious and expectant looks. A beautiful young woman remains seated at the table for a long time. In front of her is a pile of gold pieces, selecting one after another she places them upon the figures. The pile of gold increases, when suddenly by an unlucky turn of the card it is all won from her, and she calmly rises, bids her friends good evening and retires, portraying no discomforture at her loss. One lady nearly eighty years old, very richly attired, with trembling hands places upon the figure, not a single piece but a roll of sovereigns, she loses and wins alternately, at no time putting down less than one hundred dollars, and when we came away she was still anxiously playing at *Rouge-et-noir*.

For shame! that any civilized government should legalize and tolerate this wicked practice, especially in a place where the young and innocent are liable to be tempted and fall into the snare.

Shady glens, retired walks, terraced hills, and silver streams, allure one for hours to, linger amid their fascinating and enrapturing beauties.

After a refreshing shower we are seated upon the veranda of our hotel. The scarlet vines which completely cover the trellis-work of the veranda are dazzling with innumerable gem-like rain drops glistening in the setting sun. The rosy flush gradually fades away from the distant mountains of the Black Forest, until twilight changes to the gray of evening.

To-day is a gala-day here. Flags are flying from the old and new *schloss*, both castles crowning the town. It is the Prince of Prussia's birthday. The Crown Prince is staying here and the Queen of Prussia, Princess Alice and Louis of Hesse, and others have already arrived to celebrate the day. We are thus afforded an opportunity to see Queen Augusta, now Empress. She is tall, and comely looking, wearing a long train of costly black silk, she moves with stately step and every action is dignified, and her mild face beams with kindness.

The Crown Prince and Princess appear to enter cheerfully into the spirit of the hour.

Our stay here has been pleasant and interesting, but the time has arrived to depart. This morning we drive to the railway station where there was a great commotion. Large loads of trunks and carriages filled with attendants announce the presence of royalty; for the rank of persons in Europe is indicated, while traveling, by the number of servants and the amount of luggage which they take along with them. The royal family begin to arrive and enter a magnificent railway carriage appropriated to their use. We accompanied them on the same train as far as Kehl where the palatial car was switched off and the royal company went down the Rhine, while we crossed the river to Strasbourg.

STRASBOURG CATHEDRAL.

CHAPTER XLVIII.

STRASBOURG.

THE Cathedral of Strasbourg, and the wonderful clock which it contains, form together the greatest attraction of the city, and during the year bring thousands of sightseeing people to Strasbourg.

The *munster*, as it is called by the citizens, was commenced by Erwin of Steinbach, in the thirteenth century, who died long before it was completed; in fact it was not finished until the seventeenth century. The spire is the highest in the world, and is over twenty feet higher than the great Pyramid of Cheops in Egypt. It is a marvelous piece of architecture, being composed entirely of stone, which is cut with such precision that when you approach the city the spire resembles lace-work.

The interior is vast and imposing. There are three separate services being held in various parts of the cathedral. We make our way through the crowd to a small side door, where a fee is required of us, and we ascend the winding and worn stone stairway to the roof, from which a wide perspective of the city and country around greets our eyes. Looking down from the dizzy height, persons walking along the streets appear like the merest insects. For a small sum an old man offers us books descriptive of the view; also, photographs of the munster and spire. Near the bell-tower are inserted tablets on which are inscribed the names of the different sovereigns who have intrepidly undergone the ascent of the spire. I deem it not at all unbecoming to receive such an honor, as it is fatiguing and attended with some danger. I am asked by the watchman in the bell-tower to pull a small wire, which invitation I accepted. In an instant, as if by magic, all the cathedral bells as well as others over the city commenced such a ringing that I was momentarily alarmed at what I had done; but the watchman assured me it was opportune and all right, as it was the hour for ringing the chimes. They are all set in motion by this little wire.

Descending to the nave of the cathedral, we obtain by the payment of two or three francs a favorable position in front of the marvelous clock. As it is near the hour of twelve, people begin to assemble until some three hundred are gathered to see it and hear it strike the hour of noon.

This curious piece of mechanism is a complete astronomical almanac, showing the revolutions of the heavenly bodies, their positions at any given time, and the various changes which they undergo for hundreds of years. At midnight, before January first, the machinery sets this calendar for the year. In the lower compartment are figures of a child, a youth, a man of middle age, an old man, and of death. Every quarter of an hour these step forward in their order, from youth to old age, and strike the bell, after which they retire. Every day at twelve o'clock Death strikes the hour with a bone, after which, in regular procession, the twelve apostles come forth and march in front of a figure of the Savior, whose hand is extended to bless them. As they pass, each one turns and bows to him, while he acknowledges their obeisance by an inclination of the head. When Peter comes forth, a gilded rooster perched above the clock flaps his wings and crows three times, which loudly echoes through the vast building.

There are also seven figures representing the seven planets, and each day one of these emerge, while the others remain concealed until their respective turn.

The whole structure is over sixty feet in height, and was invented between the years 1837 and 1842. Before this there had been two other remarkable clocks, built in the same place, but none comparable to the present one, which has been the pride and boast of Strasbourg for the past thirty years. In a house near the cathedral is shown the model from which the clock was made.

From here we go to the church of St. Thomas, which contains the superbly chiseled monument of

Marshal Saxe. erected to his memory by Louis the Fifteenth.

Strasbourg is built upon a plain, and is strongly fortified. Around the city runs a deep moat which can be easily flooded with water. Formerly a German city, it was taken from Germany by the French under Louis the Fourteenth, in the year 1681. It has lately again been subject to the fortunes of war, and belongs once more to the Germans. The people are German in their characteristics, although they speak the French language. The houses are quaint-looking, having high and steep roofs in which are frequently to be seen seven and eight rows of dormer windows. The women go without bonnets, wearing merely a huge bow of either plain black or plaid ribbon on their heads.

At the Hotel D'Angleterre we meet some Americans, which suggests thoughts of home and of those we have been so long absent from. We take the cars, which in a few hours set us down in Mayence, where we rest preparatory to sailing down the Rhine.

CHAPTER XLIX.

DOWN THE RHINE.

"A blending of all beauties; streams and dells,
Fruit, foliage, crag, wood, cornfield, mountain, ruin,
And chiefless castles breathing stern farewells
From gray but leafy walls, where ruin greenly dwells."

THE most charming and interesting views on the German's favorite river are between Mayence and Cologne. Here we see ivy-covered ruins of old castles crowning almost every mountain. Small steamers ply daily up and down the lovely river, which are well patronized, not only by the residents of the villages, towns, and cities along the Rhine, but by strangers from many lands.

Mayence, or Mainz as the Germans call it, is a place of no small importance. It has a powerful garrison, and is near to Wiesbaden, the celebrated German watering place, from which on pleasant afternoons much company is attracted to Mayence to listen to the performance of the military bands. Gutenberg, the inventor of printing was born here in 1397. A superior monument of him by Thorwaldsen stands in front of the theatre in Gutenberg-Platz. There is one name especially honored by the ladies of Mainz, and that is *Meissen*, the minstrel called *Frausnlbe*, or woman lover, because he made the virtues of women the theme of his songs. In 1843 the ladies of Mainz erected a monument to his memory.

The remains of a Roman aqueduct in Mainz prove the great antiquity of the city. In the 8th century St. Boniface was archbishop of Mainz, which was even then a flourishing town. The celebrated sparkling hock is made in Mayence, and there are great manufactories of leather, pottery, furniture, carriages, and pianos; a most valuable and extensive library, and among museums one of

Roman antiquities. One collection contains the wonderful astronomical clock by Alexius Johann.

We engage our passage down the Rhine, stopping first at Biebrich, where we see the palace of the Duke of Nassau. Then, Rudesheim, where is founded the legend of the lovely Gisela. Next, Bingen, which is charmingly situated at the mouth of the river Nahe, and has been made memorable by Mrs. Norton's beautiful poem,

> "On the vine-clad hills of Bingen,
> Fair Bingen on the Rhine."

Near here is the celebrated Tower of Bishop Hatto. I cannot refrain from making room for the tradition so movingly described by Southey.

> "The summer and autumn hath been so wet,
> That in winter the corn was growing yet
> 'T was a piteous sight to see all around
> The grain lie rotting on the ground.
>
> Every day the starving poor
> Crowded around Bishop Hatto's door,
> For he had a plentiful last year's store;
> And all the neighborhood could tell
> His granaries were furnish'd well.

At last Bishop Hatto appointed a day
To quiet the poor without delay:
He bade them to his great barn repair,
And they should have food for the winter there.

Rejoiced at such tidings, good to hear,
The poor folk flock'd from far and near;
The great barn was full as it could hold
Of women and children, and young and old.

Then, when he saw it could hold no more,
Bishop Hatto he made fast the door;
And while for mercy on Christ they call,
He set fire to the barn and burnt them all.

'I' faith, 'tis an excellent bonfire!' quoth he,
'And the country is greatly obliged to me
For ridding it, in these times forlorn,
Of rats that only consume the corn.'

So then to his palace returned he,
And he sat down to his supper merrily,
And he slept that night like an innocent man;
But Bishop Hatto never slept again.

In the morning, as he entered the hall,
Where his picture hung against the wall,
A sweat like death all o'er him came,
For the rats had eaten it out of the frame.

As he look'd there came a man from his farm;
He had a countenance white with alarm:
'My lord, I open'd your granaries this morn,
And the rats had eaten all your corn.'

Another came running presently,
And he was as pale as pale could be:
'Fly! my lord bishop, fly!' quoth he;
'Ten thousand rats are coming this way;
The Lord forgive you for yesterday!'

'I'll go to my tower on the Rhine,' replied he;
''Tis the safest place in Germany;
The walls are high and the shores are steep,
And the stream is strong, and the water deep!'

Bishop Hatto fearfully hasten'd away,
And he cross'd the Rhine without delay,
And reach'd his tower and barr'd with care
All the windows, doors, and loop-holes there.

He laid him down and closed his eyes,
But soon a scream made him arise;
He started, and saw two eyes of flame
On his pillow, from whence the screaming came.

He listened and look'd: it was only the cat;
But the bishop he grew more fearful for that;
For she sat screaming, mad with fear,
At the army of rats that were drawing near.

For they have swum over the river so deep,
And they have climb'd the shores so steep;
And now, by thousands, up they crawl
To the holes and windows in the wall.

Down on his knees the bishop fell,
And faster and faster his beads did he tell,
As louder and louder, drawing near,
The saw of their teeth without, he could hear.

And in at the windows and in at the door,
And through the walls by thousands they pour,
And down through the ceiling, and up through the floor,
From the right and the left, from behind and before.
From within and without, from above and below—
And all at once to the bishop they go.

They have whetted their teeth against the stones,
And now they pick the bishop's bones;
They gnaw'd the flesh from every limb,
For they were sent to do judgment on him."

At St. Goarhausen is a singular grotto, where a noise like the blast of a bugle or the firing of a gun causes fifteen distinct echoes to be returned.

The scenery from here to St. Goar is wild and majestic. A short distance below is the extensive fortress of Rheinfels, which was blown up by the French in 1794.

Boppart now comes in sight. It is an ancient town of Roman origin. Before reaching Coblenz, on the left, we come to Stolzenfels, a splendid castle belonging to the Emperor of Prussia, and where he entertained Queen Victoria and Prince Albert in magnificent style in 1845.

Coblenz is the capital of Rhenish Prussia, and is situated at the mouth of the Moselle. It was built by the Romans, who called it "Confluentia." Here the grandsons of Charlemagne met to divide his great empire into France, Germany, and Italy. It is the birth-place of Madam Sontag, the great *prima donna*, who died in Mexico in 1854. From a place near here is procured the celebrated Seltzer water.

Across the river is situated the vast rocky fortress of Ehrenbreitstein. The fortifications of Coblenz give it the title of the Gibraltar of the Rhine. It is said to have been founded by the Romans under Julian, and in the Thirty Years War it was a place of great strategetical importance. The magazines will hold provisions enough to support 8000 men ten years; while the cisterns on the platform at the top will hold water enough to last three years.

We are again in motion, and as we approach Neuwied a thick fog surrounds us, which obliterates the fine view, and compels the captain to come to anchor in the middle of the river.

It was noon of the next day before our little steamer could navigate the channel again in safety. Again in motion, we passed Nuns' Island, on which rests the castle of Rolandseck, where Roland so often cast his sorrowful eyes, while his betrothed was so many years imprisoned there.

On the right, towering up to the sky, is the rugged Dragon's Rock, or Drachenfels, so called from the legend of a dragon which once inhabited a cavern in the side of the rock. Perched on the summit is a ruined castle which was so long the home of the robber chiefs of the Rhine, and which has been enchantingly described by Byron—

"The castled crag of Drachenfels
Frowns o'er the wide and winding Rhine."

The last important town before reaching Cologne is Bonn, founded by the Empress Helena, mother of Constantine, in the year 320. In this town there is a fine bronze statue of the Empress, also one of Beethoven, and the house in which he resided. Bonn has a famous University and the finest and most extensive university buildings, perhaps, in all Europe. It has a library containing 140,000 volumes, a museum of antiquities, an archæological collection, a cabinet of natural history, and a large riding academy in the basement. It has a distinct building for anatomy ; and its botanical gardens, its zoölogical and mineralogical collections are a full mile away. It has also an astronomical observatory and a fine agricultural academy, while catholic and protestant students have different divinity schools. The number of professors and tutors is about one hundred. From Bonn down the river to Cologne is but a short distance. The Rhine is to the Germans what the Nile is to the Egyptians. The people along the country through which it runs are apparently thrifty and happy. Every foot of the soil is under cultivation, even to the sides of the mountains, which are terraced and planted with vineyards. It being the time of the vintage, we have seen hundreds vigorously employed gathering grapes for making the much prized Rhine wine. Among others, we saw the famous vineyards of Rudesheim, Johannisberger, and Hockheimer.

The shores of the Rhine abound with towers, castles, crags, and fortresses, around which cling legends and fabulous traditions, all dear to the German mind, and romantically interesting to tourists, especially those interested in the history and the literature of Germany.

CHAPTER L.

COLOGNE.

WE are assigned pleasant rooms in the Hotel de Hollande looking out upon the Rhine. The windows are double like two glass doors which open sideways instead of moving up and down. A handsome porcelain stove with white ground and colored figures stands in the corner. The floor is laid in patterns of polished oak. The walls are painted with ornamental designs and the furniture is in keeping with the decorations. While seated in this room looking out upon the dark waters of the Rhine, the moon slowly rose from behind the distant hills, throwing its silver light upon the wide sweeping river whose ripples broke it into ten thousand sparkling diamonds.

I am awakened from my musing by the ringing of a bell. It was a servant presenting several cards, on which were written names of commissioners for the most desirable and reliable establishments to buy *eau de cologne*, etc.

This being a bright clear and invigorating morning we drive to the house No. 10 Sternengasse in which Peter Paul Rubens was born in 1577. Maria de Medici died in the same house in 1642. In one of the rooms are a few of the earliest works of the master, among them a painting of a child and kitten, the price of which was four thousand dollars.

On the front of the house is a portrait of Rubens wearing a low crowned, broad brimmed hat decorated with an ostrich plume.

From here we are guided to the celebrated church of St. Ursula.

Knocking at the door of the church of St. Ursula containing the bones of eleven thousand virgins, we are admitted by a woman. In the walls overhead, in the pavement and everywhere we look are glass cases filled with these unsightly bones.

The legend of Saint Ursula is a grim and terrible one, daughter of a Christian Prince of Britain, she was demanded in marriage by a Pagan Prince whom she abhorred; but, fearing the results of refusing him she pretended to consent on condition that she might have a delay of three years, a grant of money and ten noble companions, each, as well as herself, attended by one thousand virgins. The three years were passed mostly in nautical exercises, and when the nuptial day arrived Saint Ursula and her companions prayed for a storm, which arose duly and wafted them to the mouth of the Rhine and then up to Basle, where they left their ships and went on foot to Rome. When returning to Cologne they fell in with the Huns who murdered them all because Ursula refused to marry their leader. The people of Cologne buried their bodies and subsequently built a church in honor of the Virgin Martyrs.

The Cathedral at Cologne is one of the most magnificent Gothic monuments in the world. The heart of Maria de Medici is buried under a slab in the pavement. The cathedral has on the exterior a double range of flying buttresses and intervening piers and a wilderness of richly wrought pinnacles. I walked with reverence amid its lofty arches and columns which arose high and far above me, lighted up ethereally by the light streaming through the painted glass windows.

This colossal pile was commenced in 1248, and is not yet completed. Probably it never will be finished according to the original plan, as the name even of its first architect is lost, and as it is estimated that it will require over five millions of dollars to finish the structure. There is a legend in Cologne that Satan, who became jealous at the vastness of the undertaking, vowed that it should never be completed; and hence the delay from century to century is the result of his wicked scheming.

Everywhere we go we are importuned by agents, whose business it is to call upon all strangers who visit Cologne to recommend to them the only place where the genuine cologne can be obtained. There are some sixteen or seventeen manufactories all claiming to be the original inventors of this well known perfume. There are Maria Farina, Johann Farina, Anton Maria Farina, Johanna Anton Farina, and several other Farina's. All exhibiting medals, and official stamps declaring the cologne which they offer to be the *bona fide* article. These agents cling to you with pertinacity, expecting you to make an extravagant purchase of them. It is conceded by travelers that the people along the river suppose, "*Die Englandier haben viel gelt*"—the Englishman has lots of money.

The country from Cologne to Aix la Chapelle is no exception to the rest of German scenery. Every little patch of land is tilled. The women as well as the men are toiling in the fields. They tramp about in heavy wooden shoes conveying upon their heads baskets filled with vegetables.

Invalids gather at Aix la Chapelle to drink the water of its warm sulphur springs. The air is pure and the climate healthy. At the principal hotel a band of music is employed every day.

The next place of attraction before reaching

Brussels is Liege, owing to its extensive iron manufactories, termed the Birmingham of Belgium. As we enter the city at night, the country for miles around is illuminated with a hundred flames bursting from the chimneys of its great factories, presenting the appearance of a city on fire.

From here to Brussels the distance is seventy miles through a delightful country. In the railway carriage we become acquainted with a Russian gentleman and two ladies who were on their way from St. Petersburg to Paris. As soon as they ascertained that we were Americans they became quite sociable and made many inquiries about our country. They spoke English fluently, and evidently belonged to the higher classes of Russian society.

I was much interested when they began to describe a visit of some Americans last summer to their Emperor at his palace on the Black Sea, which created no little sensation among the people of St. Petersburg. Most of their papers had published the address which was presented to the Emperor, and the names of the *Quaker City* passengers, which were attached to it.

After their glowing description we informed them that we were cognizant of the event to which they had been alluding, and that we had had the pleasure of forming part of the Emperor's guests.

CHAPTER LI.

BRUSSELS AND WATERLOO.

ALTHOUGH Belgium is comparatively a small nation and covers but a limited portion of Europe, I believe it ranks first on the continent in its manufactories and enterprise.

The Belgians are evidently the Yankees of Europe. In no city that we have visited is there such an air of neatness, splendor, and smartness, as in Brussels. It has many elegant buildings. The streets are wide and at night brilliantly lighted. This fair city is quite a resting place for travelers going from England and France to the Rhine. The air at all times of the year is clear and bracing, which makes it a desirable and healthy residence for persons of delicate constitution.

The houses are built after the manner of those in Paris, and the French language is spoken throughout the city although the Flemish is the native tongue.

The Palace of Leopold, the King, is an elegant structure and superbly furnished. Near by is the one that was presented to the Prince of Orange by the city of Brussels, and afterward occupied by him, and the Old Palace, which was at one period the richest of all the palaces of Europe. The Hotel de Ville is a magnificent specimen of Gothic architecture adorned with many statues. In front of it is the statue of the Crusader, Godfrey de Bouillon. On one side of the Place Royale is the handsome building of Parliament erected by Maria Theresa.

There are many pleasure-inviting parks. In the one fronting the capital we enjoy the music of a band which plays here every day.

The Museum is exceedingly interesting. Here we see the works of the old Flemish school of art, also those of the modern masters. The "Deluge," by Corribers, "The Song of Angels," by Paul Veronese, and "Christ bearing the Cross," by Rubens, are among the most admired in the galleries.

Among the churches St. Gudule stands preëminent. Our intelligent guide points out the strangely yet beautifully carved pulpit, and the matchless stained glass windows, as ranking above all others.

Of course we gave some time to the world-renowned lace manufactories. In large rooms lighted by windows painted white, we see between thirty and forty women and girls bending over cushions in which are innumerable extremely fine needles. From these points which are kept crossing and recrossing until the whole seems an intricate mass of the finest conceivable threads, come forth the sprigs, buds and flowers of the costly and rich lace. One of the work-women informed me that it was so injurious to the eyes that they could not work at lace making over ten years, as at the end of that time their eye-sight begins to be impaired. In the sales-room point-lace over-dresses, veils, shawls, sacks, and trimmings were exhibited. It appeared almost incredible that they were manufactured in such a wearisome manner. Some of the articles require the labor of two or three women several months.

Point lace, or *point à l'agnille* is made entirely with the needle; and after the *point d'Alençon* and the famous *point de Venise*, which is not now manufactured, ranks the highest in value. The *point appliqué* is made by sewing sprigs of real point lace upon a plain net, while in the real point lace, the mesh and all are made at the same time. The *point d'Alençon* is made of pure, hand-spun linen thread which is worth from five hundred to six hundred dollars a pound. Some English writer says that Honiton lace owes its popularity to Queen Victoria, who commiserating the sad condition of the Devon lace makers determined to aid them; and to this end had her wedding lace of Honiton, which immediately brought it into fashion, and it has continued expensive ever since.

Many of the houses of Brussels have mirrors suspended above their windows in such a manner that those within can see reflected all that is going on in the street without being seen themselves.

In front of the Grande Bretagne the carriage is waiting to convey us twelve miles to the battlefield of Waterloo. Our course is through the *Alloe Verte* with its great trees and interlacing branches. Here the *élite* of Belgium's capital take their evening ride. For a long distance we drive beneath shade trees planted on either side of the road. Arriving at the village of Waterloo, the little tavern was pointed out where Wellington stayed part of the night before the famous struggle. Here he and his chief officers decided to attend the Duchess of Richmond's ball to prevent sudden surprise in the city of Brussels. They attended the ball as if nothing important was transpiring. Wellington left at midnight, and before morning all the divisions had broken up their encampments, and were on the march to meet the French.

Our driver halts to give us time to go inside of the chapel containing monuments to the memory of the distinguished officers who fell during the battle. Approaching Waterloo, on the right we pass the cottage where resided Victor Hugo, and where he wrote his matchless description of the engagement.

Here commences a strife among the guides to see who should be employed. One declared that his father was in the battle, another that his grandfather was one of Napoleon's generals. Finally one presents a well written letter from Victor Hugo, recommending him and verifying the fact that this guide accompanied Hugo through all his studious wanderings of many weeks over the ground. Admitting the truth of the old saying "the last is the best," we employed him and were soon climbing up the steps of the lofty and victorious mound, on the summit of which is a colossal lion looking toward France. The guide now takes his position facing the north, and commences his description. Turning gradually to the east, south, and west he pours forth a torrent of words, stopping every little while to take breath. His speech would have done credit to a Sumner or a Disraeli.

"There stands the Hougoumont. To the right La Haye Sainte. Yonder swept down the brave Highlanders carrying everything before them. In that deep ditch fell the fiercely charging French unseen by their commander, until it was filled with men and horses forming a level surface over which charged the contending armies. That distant rise of ground was taken and retaken four or five times. Where we stand the Prince of Orange fell wounded. That monument is the place where the courageous Hanoverians struggled. The other one marks the death of Colonel Gordon.

Along that road came Napoleon galloping, sure that he had carried the day. Over those distant woods rolled the dust of Blucher's swiftly advancing army whose presence decided the struggle." Thus the description went on. The speaker becoming more and more eloquent, his voice growing louder and his manner more excited until we almost fancied that we heard the roar of cannon and actually saw the smoke of the battle.

It was the unanimous opinion that our guide

had well earned his five francs, from each one, which was willingly paid him.

After a limited time in the Museum, filled with relics of Waterloo, we journey back to Brussels.

CHAPTER LII.

ANTWERP AND THE NORTH SEA.

ANTWERP being the last place of our sojourn on the Continent, a few days will be devoted to this antique city, and then good-bye to the palaces, cathedrals, and galleries of art, of the Old World. Our journey through Scotland and Ireland will be rapid, the main purpose being to observe the condition and characteristics of the people and the scenery of the two countries.

Antwerp was an ancient city at the height of its prosperity three or four centuries ago, when it was the first commercial city of Europe, having sometimes two and three thousand ships of all nations in its harbor at once, and a population of some 200,000. In 1576 it was sacked by the Spaniards, and burned. In 1588 it was captured by Prince

Alexander of Parma, and two hundred years after, it fell into the hands of the French.

Although the greatness of this once powerful city has departed, it still contains much that cannot fail to instruct and interest the tourist. There are fine collections of the works of Rubens and Vandyck. The latter was born here. The celebrated chef d'œuvre, *The Descent from the Cross*, in the Cathedral, painted by Rubens, is one of the finest by that master. The life-like appearance of all the figures, and the naturalness of their positions as they tenderly lower the Savior from the cross, cannot be surpassed. In the square fronting our hotel is a well executed statue of the immortal painter, and on the Rue de Rubens is the house where Rubens died. As we wander through the handsome church of St. Jaques, and come to the vault containing Rubens and his family, I cannot but be impressed with the thought that although nearly three hundred years have intervened since the master painter was born, his works still live, and bear over the world the inextinguishable fame of the artist.

While in the Cathedral of Notre Dame, a funeral procession enters and marches under the lofty arches of this grand and solemn temple. The organ sends forth its sublime music, while the choir responds to its tones. As they approach the high altar, on which flicker dim lights, and deposit the burial case, the throng falls back on either side, and remains transfixed, while the solemn requiem is recited for the repose of the dead.

The house of Charles the Fifth, like many others in Antwerp, is a grotesque combination of architecture, with high gables tapering to a pinnacle in which are six, and sometimes seven rows of windows. The façade of the houses are adorned with quaint old tracery dating back to the days when the Spaniards were the rulers.

I am much pleased with the markets and amused with the market women, who are so oddly dressed. They wear on their heads a comically shaped bonnet, being made of straw, the front turned up and lined, and a cape of straw with a very broad ribbon placed on plainly above it. In traveling one will continually come in contact with the sublime and ridiculous. The markets here, as in most of the European cities, are in the open squares, and when all the stands and wagons are piled high with tempting fruits and fresh vegetables, I am reminded of the horticultural fairs and festivals in my own native country. Every article is handled with that care and neatness which we have observed in all the markets since landing in Austria.

To-night, while sitting in my room, a soft and gentle voice commenced singing sweetly beneath the window. It rose and died away upon the evening air like music from some fairy land. One after another plaintive German air was breathed forth. Throwing up the sash, I saw in the dim light of the street lamp a poorly clad woman looking wistfully at my window. Money was a poor reward, for that sweet voice will ever linger around me, although I shall never hear the street singer of Antwerp again.

After viewing the King's Palace, we take passage on a small iron steamer, and glide down between the level shores of the Scheldt, out upon the German Ocean, on our way to Newcastle on the Tyne.

The afternoon is fair and lovely, and as the declining sun sinks beneath the western horizon, we have only thoughts of a pleasant voyage. About midnight a violent commotion on board told us that a gale had sprung up, and our little steamer was struggling with a heavy sea.

To-day is a gloomy Sunday; the gale has been increasing all day, until it blows a hurricane. Our captain informs us that the sails are blown to shreds, and the steamer is laboring heavily. He also tells us that he dare not approach the shores of England as long as the gale is blowing, and we are therefore heading out to sea. An attempt was made by the captain to eat his dinner, sitting on the floor of the cabin; but a heavy sea striking the ship, he was rolled with the dishes and dinner into one corner of the room. All night long the furious gale continued, and there was some fear expressed by the officers that we would not ride out the storm.

The third day the wind subsided, and we approached the coast and sailed up the busy Tyne, thankful that we had arrived in safety.

The North Sea is noted for its severe storms, and this one has been of unusual severity. The English papers were filled for days with accounts of terrible shipwrecks and loss of life along the coast of England during this gale.

We are once more in an English city, as the smoke and immense iron manufactories indicate. There are many massive and elegant buildings in Newcastle, but all are darkly colored and their beauty spoiled by the everlasting smoke. After one day's rest here, we take the cars for Melrose Abbey, Abbotsford, Edinburgh, and the Highlands of Scotland.

CHAPTER LIII.

SCOTLAND.

AT twelve o'clock we leave Newcastle. Passing swiftly by the Duke of Northumberland's place, we are soon surrounded by Scottish scenery. The fields are divided by hawthorn hedges or low stone walls, and the green velvety hills abound with flocks. In each farm-yard are numbers of hay-stacks put up with care and crossed with ropes. Humble cottages are scattered along the way.

At length the ancient Abbey of Melrose became visible in the distance. This famous *auld* abbey, made illustrious by the description in Walter Scott's "Lay of the Last Minstrel," stands upon the banks of the Tweed. One cannot but admire the venerable ruin. It is one of the choicest specimens of the gothic style. There are remains of splendid carvings, and its *gargoyles* and *corbels* still retain their position and perfect workmanship. The floor is of grass, and the sky is the roof. There are traces of the cloisters and of the monastic buildings. This was the favorite resort of Sir Walter Scott, who copied many of its quaint gargoyles for the decoration of Abbotsford, his beautiful residence. The roofless walls of Melrose Abbey are many of them thickly overgrown with ivy, and the appearance of the ruin by moonlight is dreamy and romantic in the extreme.

From Melrose to Abbotsford is a pleasant drive of three or four miles. Arriving in the vestibule, you see on a table a huge hand-bell which you ring if you are hardy enough, and a servant appears to conduct you through the fine mansion of Sir Walter. He is an excellent guide, possessing the most rare qualifications of those officials — he knows when to hold his tongue — and is withal so full of information, and so polite and gentlemanly, that you feel almost ashamed to offer him a fee for his services.

He takes it of course, and thanks you, not seeming wounded in his dignity in the least. So accustomed is the tourist to giving sixpences and shillings that he hardly knows when it is proper to omit the custom. One irreverent countryman of mine, being on Windsor Terrace when the Queen and one of the princesses took an airing there, declared that his first impulse was to offer her majesty a shilling, which he declared he was fully persuaded would be received with the inevitable smile and "thank you, sir."

Abbotsford was once an old cloister, but the present house and grounds are entirely the work of Sir Walter It is surrounded by beautiful scenery, and the interior of the mansion is rich in collections of armor and fine paintings, and the library is very extensive and valuable. The place is now occupied by the only surviving grand-daughter of the great writer. In the library there are elegant glass cases filled with curiosities and presents from distinguished persons — among them a splendid snuff-box from Napoleon I. Over the library door is a picture of Mary,

Queen of Scots, after she was beheaded—that is, a picture of the severed head. It is far less "prettified" than most of the representations of her, and strikes the beholder at once as a true portrait. While looking at this life-like portrait, and reflecting upon the cares of the unfortunate Mary, I must confess that there is that in the expression of the face which speaks eloquently to the hearts of sympathizers with the unhappy queen.

Leading out from the library on the right is the private study of Sir Walter, with his leather-covered chair and table just as he last used them. Near the table is a chair made from the wood of the house where Wallace was betrayed. This study is richly furnished to the ceiling with books, approached by an elegant iron staircase leading to galleries that extend all around the room. At the left as you enter the study is a very small room or closet which Sir Walter called his "*speak-a-bit.*" In this is a cast of his head taken after death. The one thing noticeable about this cast, and ever to be remembered, is the extraordinary length of the upper lip. The head, as everybody knows, is extremely high, but not wide in proportion. The guide offered stereoscopic views of this bust which I have never seen for sale anywhere else.

This morning the Scotch mist is falling, but it does not prevent our seeing the city of Edinburgh.

Edinburgh abounds with historic associations dear to the heart of every Scotchman. It is truly a grand city. From Calton Hill the finest view is afforded. Princes street, with its elegant stores and hotels, stretches far away through the center of Edinburgh.

In a prettily laid-out square on Princes street is the lofty gothic monument of Sir Walter Scott, adorned with scenes in high relief from his romances. Meg Merrilies is of course the most striking of the characters, and the figure is admirably done.

Towering high above the city on the summit of a rock from four to five hundred feet perpendicular height, is Edinburgh Castle. This is an ancient fortress erected by Edward the Second, of England, and many times in the history of this fortress have the flags of Scotland and of England floated alternately from its tower. This rock and fortress give the town a very picturesque appearance. Edinburgh is often called the "Athens of Scotland."

We walk down Cannongate street to the house of John Knox. Over the door is the following inscription: "Love the Lord above all, and thy neighbor as thyself." The great reformer is buried in the cemetery of St. Giles Cathedral. His house is a dilapidated looking building, and at one of the windows is a figure representing him, and indicating the place from which he preached to the populace.

The University is one of the finest in Europe, and has in its library nearly one hundred and fifty thousand volumes.

Edinburgh has numerous churches, many of which are well known in America, through their earnest and able preachers who have occupied our pulpits at various times.

Holyrood Palace is a massive old structure, well identified with the history of Scotland. In its galleries are the mythical portraits of one hundred and six Scottish Kings. The most important of all the rooms is the one once occupied by Mary, Queen of Scots. We are told that everything we see is just as it was placed by herself. On a small table is her work-box embroidered with silk, the design being Jacob's Ladder. This the unfortunate Mary worked when she was but twelve years of age. The covering of the chairs were also needle-worked by her. Beside the bed stands the infant basket of her son, James the Sixth. Her dressing room is hung with old tapestry, and in another room is the stone on which Darnley and the beautiful Mary knelt when they were married. Another room is pointed out as the one where Rizzio was murdered. The blood stains are still shown. Here also is the chamber where King James was aroused from his sleep at midnight, by the swift-flying courier who informed him of the death of Queen Elizabeth. What memories cluster around one while visiting these old castles and palaces in Scotland and England! England is a great and powerful nation, and at present her government is one of the wisest and best upon the earth; but what a history have England and Scotland! The strifes, envies, jealousies, and ambitions of her Kings and Queens have been the cause of crimes and sufferings enough to appall the stoutest heart.

To-day is Sunday, and as the bells toll the hour of service everything breathes a spirit of calm repose. Old and young are wending their way slowly to the *kirks*.

> "Slowly the throng moves o'er the tomb-paved ground,
> The aged man, the bowed down, the blind,
> Led by the thoughtless boy, and he who breathes
> With pain, and eyes the new-made grave well pleased;
> These, mingled with the young, the gay, approach
> The house of God; these, spite of their ills,
> A glow of gladness feel; with silent praise
> They enter in; a placid stillness reigns
> Until the man of God, worthy the name,
> Opens the book and reverentially
> The stated portion reads."

The preacher has made a solemn and effective appeal both morning and afternoon; and as the congregation quietly disperse each one wears a look of Christian thoughtfulness, showing that the lessons of the hour have not been unheeded.

The sun is going down, but its golden light still lingers upon the uplands, and as night spreads her sable mantle, it closes a day whose hours have been full, rich, and peaceful—my first Sunday in Christian Scotland.

CHAPTER LIV.

FROM SCOTLAND AND IRELAND, HOME.

THE famous Highlands of Scotland are more interesting to lovers of Scott's romances and songs than to others. There is hardly a lake, or mountain, or glen not immortalized by him. "Ellen's Isle," "Lanrick Mead," "The Trossack's Gorge," and numberless other places connected with *The Lady of the Lake* and other works of his, are eagerly visited by travelers. The mountains, Ben Nevis, Ben Avon, Ben Lomond, Ben-y-Gloe and the numerous lakes or lochs are visited by stage coaches during the summer. The scenery is grand and wild. From the Highlands and the Highlanders, the lochs and bens, we arrive at Glasgow by the Caledonian railway. Glasgow is very different in appearance from Edinburgh. It is located upon the banks of the Clyde, and is the chief commercial city of Scotland. In one of the squares is a fine equestrian statue of Queen Victoria and one of the Prince of Wales.

The Cathedral of Glasgow is surrounded with associations connecting it intimately with the history of Scotland. It now belongs to the Protestants. Surrounding it is an extensive burying ground. Among the monuments is one erected to the memory of John Knox. It is in this Cathedral that part of the scenes of Rob Roy was laid. The Royal Exchange, the Bank of Scotland, and the parks are all worthy of being visited. From Glasgow the sail down the Clyde is remarkable, from the fact that along its shores can be seen in process of construction so many of the great iron steamships which are now found on every ocean and every sea.

Bidding "*gude bye*" to the land of Robert Burns we cross the channel to Ireland. The country through which we travel is enlivening, for Ireland is not the commonplace country that some suppose. The air is delightful and invigorating. Most of the land is devoted to grazing purposes, and flocks of superior horses, cattle, and sheep are cropping the smooth tender grass. Here and there is the usual hut. It is made of stone and sometimes whitewashed. It has a thatched roof often overgrown with moss, and there is one door and generally one window. Each house has a small patch of vegetables and the inevitable pig and cow.

I can hardly realize that this small island has furnished the vast multitude of Irish emigrants which has been pouring upon the shores of America for the past fifty years.

Arriving at Dublin we find a magnificent city. Sackville street, its principal thoroughfare, almost equals Broadway, New York, the Strand or Oxford Street, London, or the Boulevards of Paris.

Dublin has many fine buildings, the Custom House on the bank of the Liffey, ranking first. Near the Bank of Ireland is the celebrated Trinity College from which have emanated some of the most learned scholars of modern times. The students wear a peculiar flat black hat, which does not add much to their appearance, but as this hat marks them as being students of Trinity College they assume much arrogance in wearing it. We attend service at St. Patrick's Cathedral. Its isles are crowded with richly-attired and well-bred people.

Dublin prides itself upon its aristocracy.

In Dublin I have my first experience in riding in the jaunting car peculiar to Ireland. The Irishman terms it "a cab with wheels inside." Holding from three to four persons they go flying up and down every street, and it requires some practice to remain comfortably seated without falling off. After inspecting Dublin castle, the residence of the Lord Lieutenant of Ireland, we call at Kildare, Limerick, Blarney Castle, and Cork.

At Cork the guide leads the way to the church of the Holy Trinity, Father Mathew's church, his statue, and the Queen's College.

From Cork we sail down the lovely "Silver Lee." On either side are the ivy and moss covered ruins of old castles and towers. We listen involuntarily for

> "The bells of Shandon
> That sound so grand on
> The pleasant waters of the Silver Lee."

Arriving at the Cove of Cork, or Queenstown as it is now called, we remain for two days at the Queen's Hotel, our windows looking out upon one of the finest harbors in the world.

This clear and crisp November morning we see the powerful steamer which is to bear us across the ocean lying quietly at anchor in the offing.

Going on board we find our stateroom in order awaiting our coming, having been secured in Liverpool by telegraph.

Through storm and calm we are borne swiftly back to our native land, and my great journey is ended. As I lay down my pen I may add that through all the different countries which we have traveled, whether among the sturdy Britons or the hardy Alpine mountaineers, the happy Germans or the more reserved Russians, among the swarthy Turks and Egyptians and even among the wild Arabs of Syria, we have been kindly received.

Access has been granted us to palaces and private residences of the Old World and the more sacred places of the Orient, simply because we were Americans.

I am grateful that it has been my fortune and pleasure to have seen this majestic and sublime panorama of the different nations, kindred, and tongues of the world; and the lessons and experiences which I have learned, will go with me until I am called to start on that inevitable and mysterious journey from which no messages are sent back and from which no traveler ever returns.

" Cœlum non animum mutant qui trans mare current."

www.ingramcontent.com/pod-product-compliance
Lightning Source LLC
Chambersburg PA
CBHW030546300426
44111CB00009B/879